BU

for

includes
DISCOUNT
COUPONS FOR
ATTRACTIONS
& MUSEUMS

e guidebook that pays for itself in one day

The *for less* Guidebook series...

- ■ 288-page guidebooks
- ■ Detailed fold-out street maps
- ■ **Discount card** that gives up to 4 people great savings at 300 of the city's best places *(attractions, museums, restaurants, shops, tours etc).*

The *for less* Compact Guide series...

- ■ 76-page guidebooks
- ■ Detailed fold-out street maps
- ■ 2-for-1 (or 50%) discounts at top attractions and museums

...PLUS 50 more for less Compact Guides to follow

Budapest
for less

Compact
Guide

Publisher Information

First published in Great Britain in 1999 by
Metropolis International (UK) Ltd.

ISBN 1 901811 65 4

COPYRIGHT

DISCLAIMER

Assessments of attractions, hotels, museums and s
forth are based on the author's impressions and
therefore contain an element of subjective opinio
that may not reflect the opinion of the publishers

The contents of this publication are believed to b
correct at the time of printing. However, details
such as opening times will change over time. We
would advise you to call ahead to confirm
important information.

All organizations offering discounts in this
guidebook have a contract with the publisher to
give genuine discounts to holders of valid *for less*
vouchers.

The publisher and/or its agents will not be
responsible if any establishment breaches its
contract (although it will attempt to secure
compliance) or if any establishment changes
ownership and the new owners refuse to honour
the contract.

Care has been taken to ensure that discounts are
only offered at reputable establishments, however
the publisher and/or its agents cannot accept
responsibility for the quality of merchandise or
service provided, nor for errors or inaccuracies in
this guidebook.

The publisher will not be held responsible for an
loss, damage, injury, expense or inconvenience
sustained by any person, howsoever caused, as a
result of information or advice contained in this
guide except insofar as the law prevents the
exclusion of such liability.

Publisher

Metropolis International
222 Kensal Road
London W10 5BN
England

Telephone:
+44-(0)20-8964-4242

Fax:
+44-(0)20-8964-4141

E-mail:
admin@for-less.com

Web site:
http://www.for-less.com

ABBREVIATIONS

☎	Telephone number
🕐	Opening times
Ⓜ	Metro station

Contents

HOW TO OBTAIN DISCOUNTS

Many of the museums and attractions in this guide offer discounts to holders of this book.

Museums and attractions which offer a discount are highlighted in pink in the text and designated by the following symbol in the margins:

To obtain your discount, simply hand in the appropriate voucher from the back of the book when you purchase your ticket.

Introduction to Budapest

Budapest, the capital of Hungary and a city of over 2 million people, is fast developing as a top destination for tourists. Its beauty and character derive from a complex history, a rich culture and its position as a city geographically situated at the crux of East and West.

Only ten years since it emerged from communist rule, Budapest today captivates the visitor with a unique blend of 19th century architecture, modern amenities and medieval ruins.

Reflections

'Looking upstream a great vista unfolds ... a canvas of great beauty matched by few cities in the world' - Field Marshal Count von Moltke, 1835

It is a city for all tastes. There are countless historical signposts to be found around town that help the visitor piece together the two-thousand-year history of revolt, rebuilding, calamity and celebration that has sculpted the city into what it is today.

For those with sufficient stamina, walking is definitely the best way to explore. Wear some comfortable shoes, for behind the gates of this elegant, timeless and fascinating city, there is plenty to see and do.

Wander between the city's grand buildings, which have seen the passing of monarchs and governments. Admire the elegant bridges that link the two old cities of Buda and Pest on either side of the Danube. Soak up the history of the ornate churches that have hosted hundreds of

Parliament viewed from the Castle District of Buda

Looking along the embankment

ears of worship. Succumb to the charm
f the pretty squares where generations of
Budapest residents have gone to walk, talk
nd relax.

here are plenty of good museums
edicated to national treasures, natural
istory, medicine and military history.

he galleries, too, are noteworthy, with
emarkable exhibits of medieval stonework,
cclesiastical relics, fine art and pop art.
hose visitors here for a longer stay will be
ble to explore quite a few of these
nstitutions, while others with less time will
ant to concentrate on a couple of the
ollections and enjoy them at their leisure.

ight owls can indulge in a wide range of
vening entertainments, from grand opera
alas to funky nightclubs, from
xperimental theatre to classical ballet.
ating out in Budapest is a delight, and a
late of Hungarian goulash washed down
ith a local wine is a must.

udapest is a city for all seasons. In
inter it can look like something from an
astern European fairytale, with the roofs
f ancient buildings in the **Castle District**
den with snow and the trees gripped
ght with frost. On a foggy morning,
astle Vajdahunyad in the **City Park** looks
erily similar to the spooky Transylvanian
rtress on which it is modelled.

the weeks before Christmas, houses,

Did You Know ...?

Hungary suffered the
world's worst ever level
of inflation after the
Second World War. Within
a year, the equivalent of
the previous value of one
pengö (the unit of
currency at the time)
increased to nearly one
and a half billion *pengös*.

Budapest from the air

shops and trees are decorated with bright lights. At weekends families can be seen ice-skating on the frozen lakes in the city's parks or taking a warm plunge in one of the many natural baths that are fed by numerous hot springs sourced from deep in the Earth. There is no shortage of charming coffeehouses, which are a welcome refuge from the sub-zero temperatures. Relax in the warmth and enjoy a piping-hot espresso and a fortifying, calorific cake.

Did You Know...?

Famous Budapest residents have included the great composers Franz Liszt and Béla Bartók.

Spring sees the return of greenery to the tree-lined streets and parks, which are popular with both tourists and locals for strolls and picnics. Watch out for the spring arts festival.

Budapest enjoys long hot summers with temperatures reaching 30°C (85°F) or more in July. Summer is the most popular time for visitors and the weather obviously enhances the pleasure of ambling through the streets and taking in the sights.

You might like to take some trips a few miles out of town, for instance to **Lake Balaton**, which is the closest this land-locked country gets to having a sea shore

If you are lucky enough to be in the city around August 20 you will be able to catch the spectacular St. Stephen's Day firework display, when rockets fired from the walls of the **Citadella** in the Castle District light up the night sky.

With the end of the summer and the start of cooler temperatures, the main arts season begins, as the opera house, theatres and music venues embark on their busy programmes of events.

Budapest is, above all, an elegant city. Its architecture – a mixture of styles evolved over the centuries – is both beautiful and fascinating. The photographers among you will marvel at the ornate design of the **Parliament** building, the imposing **Royal Palace** perched on its hill overlooking the city and the sturdy blocks of the **Chain Bridge** across the Danube. For a more up-to-date look at city life, head for the open markets, where Hungarians come to meet, chat, buy and sell.

Budapest residents are generally friendly and everyone has his or her story to tell about Communism. Some loathed it and welcomed the western free market economy with open arms. Others are more cautious, fearing the rising inequality between rich and poor and mourning the loss of strict controls that kept the country in line. Almost all, however, feel happy to be closer to the rest of Europe, and appreciate the greater freedom to travel and trade.

Finally, Budapest is a true city of romance – the 'Paris of the East'. At night, with the lights from the Royal Palace and the Chain Bridge dancing in the waters of the Danube, and the cruise boats gliding past, there is no better way to end the day than by strolling along the river.

Reflections

'No one is in a hurry in Budapest' – Grace Humphrey, 1936

IF YOU DO ONE THING . . .

1. If you visit one museum . . .
National Museum (page 31)

2. If you visit one church . . .
Matthias Church (page 16)

3. If you go to one art gallery . . .
the **National Gallery** (page 11)

4. If you go to one theatre . . .
the **Opera House** (pages 27 and 52)

5. If you walk in one park . . .
City Park (page 38)

6. If you dine in one restaurant . . .
Gundel (page 49)

7. If you go on one excursion . . .
Szentendre (page 46)

8. If you go to one shop . . .
the **Herend Shop** (page 50)

9. If you go to one nightclub . . .
Bahnhof (page 54)

10. If you visit one thermal bath . . .
Gellért Baths (page 14)

History of Budapest

The **Romans** were the first people to establish any substantial settlement in the vicinity of Budapest. They set up a strategic outpost at the celtic town of **Aquincum** in the 1st century BC. This became the capital of Pannonia province and the remains can still be seen today in **Óbuda** (page 43).

From the 5th century to the end of the 10th century, the region was controlled first by the **Huns** under **Attila**, then the **Avars** (a tribe from the east). Later, the **Magyars** invaded and established a feudal state. **Stephen I** was crowned as Hungary' first Christian king in 1000.

It was not until the 13th century that the separate settlements of Buda and Pest grew into sizeable towns. Mid-way through the century the **Mongols** invaded and razed Pest. The rest of the 13th century saw the first of Budapest's many periods of rebuilding. Under the auspices of **King Béla IV**, the construction of the fortress o Castle Hill and the Royal Palace began.

In 1541 it was the turn of the **Turks** to invade, and so began an occupation which only ended when they were expelle by the **United Christian armies** in 1686. For the next two hundred years, the city was ruled by the Habsburgs.

The period between 1825 and 1848 is known as the Age of Reform. The cities o Buda and Pest grew substantially and many of the grand national buildings still standing today were built. By 1848, thos opposed to the Habsburgs had acquired following and revolution was in the air. O March 15 the rebel poet **Sándor Petőfi** read aloud his National Song and sparke off the Revolution.

A result of this was that Hungary was made an equal partner in the Habsburg Empire, with Austro-Hungary a single nation. Freedom of religion and the press was granted, and the feudal system, which had kept the peasants as little mo than slaves to landowners, was abolished

In 1873 the cities of Buda and Pest were united. The new metropolis continued to

Reflections

'When I got tired of the noisy streets of Pest . . . I loved to wander about quaint silent Buda, where everything and everyone seemed to have stood still a couple of centuries ago' – Elizabeth Morris, 1931

Did You Know ...?

The population of Budapest, at 2 million, is one fifth of the population of the whole of Hungary.

grow and prosper as both an administrative and trading centre, becoming the fastest-growing city on the continent by the 1890s. Continental Europe's first underground railway was opened here in 1896 and the vast and magnificent Parliament building was built between 1885 and 1904.

After the First World War, the **Austro-Hungarian Empire** collapsed and a new Hungarian republic was declared in the autumn of 1918.

Though Hungary was on the side of the Germans for the first five years of the **Second World War**, Budapest's people, in particular the Jews, suffered terribly. In 1945, the **Soviet armies** of Russia first liberated and then occupied what was a broken city.

The communist party took power in 1947 and a people's republic was established in 1949. In 1956 the Hungarian uprising against the Soviet Union was brutally suppressed. Thousands died in Budapest alone and many more fled abroad. It was to be another 33 years before the Eastern Communist bloc disintegrated.

In 1990 Hungary held the first open, multi-party elections since the Second World War. Since then, Budapest has moved towards the free market capitalism of the west faster than perhaps any other Eastern European city.

Did You Know...?

At the end of the Second World War, all the bridges that spanned the Danube and linked Buda with Pest were blown up by the retreating Nazis.

Budapest is rich in architectural heritage

Buda

The Royal Palace

From its position overlooking the Danube, the vast **Royal Palace** (Budavari Palota), forms an impressive backdrop to the city. It is best viewed from across the river or from the **Chain Bridge** (Széchenyi Lánchíd), especially at night when it is lit up.

This is the former home of the Hungarian kings, and parts of the building date from the 13th century. After much wartime destruction and subsequent rebuilding, however, it contains a mixture of different architectural styles.

It is situated on **Castle Hill**, in the old fortress of the **Castle District**, whose winding streets and medieval remains joined UNESCO's list of World Heritage Sites in 1988.

The Palace houses the **Ludwig Museum** (Ludwig Múzeum), the **National Gallery** (Nemzeti Galéria), the **National Széchenyi Library** (Nemzeti Könyvtár) and the **Budapest History Museum (Budapesti Történeti Múzeum)**. *(Southern end of Castle Hill, Ⓜ Batthyány tér / Vörösmárty tér / Déli station. ⏰ – see separate museum times. Admission charge.)*

The **Budapest History Museum** takes the visitor on a journey through thousands of years of history, from the earliest Stone Age settlement, through the city's role as strategic outpost of the Roman Empire, to

Budapest History Museum

South East Wing (E) of Royal Palace
Ⓜ Batthyány tér / Vörösmarty tér / Déli station
☎ 155 8849
⏰ Nov-Feb: Wed-Mon: 10am-4pm. Tue: closed.
Mar-May 15: Wed-Mon: 10am-6pm. Tue: closed.
May 16-Sep 15: Mon-Sun: 10am-6pm. Sep 16-Oct: Wed-Mon: 10am-6pm.
Admission charge and photo permit charge.
2 admissions for the price of 1 with voucher on page 65.

he upheaval of the Second World War
nd then onto the present day. The
useum gives a fascinating and detailed
ccount of Budapest's painful and joyous
emories of invasion, communism,
volution and market capitalism. On
iew are photographs and paintings,
rtefacts and documents, maps and
harts, as well as modern visual displays.

he museum is situated in Wing E of the
oyal Palace. It was renewed in 1998 in
elebration of the 125th anniversary of
e unification of Buda, Pest and Óbuda.
cated in a renovated section of the
alace dating from medieval times, is a
ollection of artefacts that was found in
xcavations of the mid-1970s.

entre stage are the sombre Gothic
atues dating from the early 15th
entury. Apparently, they were unwanted
d thrown out into a garden, where they
y for almost 600 years until the
chaeologists dug them up.

National Gallery

e **National Gallery** holds works by some
the best known and most respected
ungarian painters and sculptors. There
e collections of Medieval and
naissance art from between the 11th
d 16th centuries, including 14th
ntury wood sculptures and 15th
ntury panel paintings and carvings.

Wings B, C and E of the
Royal Palace
Ⓜ Batthyány tér /
Vörösmarty tér /
Déli station
☎ 375 7533
🕐 Tue-Sun: 10am-6pm.
Mon: closed. Guided
tours: 11am-4pm.
Admission charge and
photo permit charge.
**2 admissions for the
price of 1 with voucher
on pages 65.**

e medieval stone carvings on display
e rare examples of Hungarian
omanesque and Gothic architecture
d sculpture. There are late
naissance and Baroque artworks from
tween 1550 and 1800, as well as more
odern collections from the 19th and
th centuries, up to 1945.

rks by two masters, Aladar Korosfoi
iesch and Sándor Nagy represent the
t Nouveau school, one of the
luences that came from western
rope. There is also a medal collection.

any of the artists on show here may not
known to visitors, but they are
portant figures within their own
untry.

see the whole collection takes more
n a day. The exhibition is so extensive

Coat of Arms above the Siklo Funicular

that it has had to be housed in three wings of the Palace. For a guided tour ca three days ahead.

The **Széchenyi Library** is the largest library in Hungary and an important national research centre. The vast building houses som several million books (estimates vary) alon with impressive collections of music scores, manuscripts and journals. Some of these have filtere down to the library from a collection that was once held by King Matthias (or Mátyás) in the latter half of the 15th century. *(Wing F of Royal Palace, Ⓜ Batthyány tér / Vörösmárty tér / Déli station, ☎ 224 3700. ⏰ Mon: 1pm-6pm. Tue-Sat: 10am-6pm. Sun: closed. Admission charge.)*

Most people arrive at or leave the Palace via the **Sikló funicular railway,** which was built in 1870. It heaves itself up the side of Castle Hill from Ádám Clark tér, a square dedicated to the Scottish enginee Adam Clark, who built the Chain Bridge (Széchenyi Lánchíd). The ride can be scary for those who suffer from vertigo, but the views are splendid and it only takes about a minute.

Funicular

Ádám Clark tér
Ⓜ Batthyány tér / Vörösmárty tér / Déli station
⏰ Mon-Sun: 7.30am-10pm. Closed every other Monday. Admission charge.

The **Ludwig Museum** is a must for lovers of modern art. You can view pieces by Picasso alongside the American pop art (Andy Warhol and Roy Lichtenstein. The museum has seen some changes over th years – it once housed the Museum of th Hungarian Workers' Movement.

It is now named after Peter and Irene Ludwig, who studied art history and philosophy at Mainz University. They began collecting ancient art in the 1950 and in the mid-1960s started buying modern works. Peter Ludwig, who died 1996, was the first serious collector of a works from the former socialist countries

The **Castle Theatre** (Várszínház) is situat

on Castle Hill near the top of the Sikló funicular railway. It was originally built in the 13th century as a church and monastery (the Order of Our Lady of Mount Carmel) but was changed from a site of religious devotion and meditation in 1787. It was the first theatre to stage a play in Hungarian. *(Színház utca 1-3, Ⓜ Batthyány tér / Vörösmárty tér / Déli station, ☎ 375 8649. Call for details of performances and prices.)*

The **Semmelweis Museum of Medical History** (Semmelweis Orvostörténeti Muzeum) is housed in the 18th-century house of Ignac Semmelweis, a doctor who invented a cure for the blood poisoning disease that killed many mothers during childbirth. His comparatively primitive equipment and anatomical models made of wax make for an unusual visit. There is also an exhibit on the methods employed in saving the wounded during the 1848-9 War of Independence.

You cannot miss the 770-foot (235-metre) **Gellért Hill** (Gellérthegy) in the centre of the city. The panoramic views across the rooftops of Budapest from the top make the steep climb worthwhile.

The hill gets its name from **Bishop Gellért**, a Venetian martyr. There is a memorial **statue** to him on the side of the hill, framed by a curved colonnade. It depicts him with his outstretched right hand clutching a cross, a symbol of his role here during the 11th century.

He helped King Stephen I spread Christianity among the Magyars and paid for it with his life when he was

Ludwig Múzeum

Wing A of Royal Palace
Ⓜ Batthyány tér /
Vörösmárty tér /
Déli station
☎ 375 7533/9175
🕐 Tue-Sun: 10am-6pm.
Mon: closed.
Guided tours by appointment.
Admission charge, credit cards not accepted.

Liberation Monument on Gellért Hill

thrown off the cliff in a barrel spiked with nails in 1046 by the pagan hordes.

Gellért Hill is an upmarket residential area and a popular place for dog-walkers and those enjoying an evening stroll.

This limestone outcrop is underscored by a fault line through which hot springs gush. These restorative waters flowing from deep inside the earth, are channelled into elaborate bathing complexes and have eased the bones of Budapest's infirm for more than 600 years.

Budapest is noted for its range of spa baths. Some are communal, some single sex, some lesbian and gay. All are wonderfully refreshing. The waters are said to ease numerous ailments, from high blood pressure to arthritis. Some of the baths are luxuriously landscaped and have indoor and outdoor pools, saunas, solariums and massage areas.

Most expensive are the **Gellért Baths,** but there are plenty of more reasonable

**Museum of
Medical History**

Apród utca 1-3
Ⓜ Ferenciek tere
☎ 375 3533
🕓 Tue-Sun: 10.30am-5.30pm.
Admission charge.

Gellért Baths

alternatives. *(Gellért at Kelenhegyi út 4,* Ⓜ *Kálvin tér,* ☎ *466 6166.* 🕓 *Mon-Sun: 6am-6pm Admission charge. Other baths: Rudas at Döbrentei tér 9,* ☎ *356 1322.* 🕓 *Mon-Fri: 6am-7pm. Sat-Sun: 6am-1pm. Jun 15-Aug 31: Sur closed. Admission charge. Király at Fo utca 84* ☎ *202 3688.* 🕓 *Open for men: Mon, Wed & Fri 6.30am-6pm. Open for women: Tue & Thu: 6.30am-6pm. Sat: 6.30am-12noon. Sun: closed. Admission charge.)*

he giant **Liberation Monument**
(Felszabadulási emlékmú), to the south,
commemorates the end of the Nazi
occupation when the Red Army marched
into the city. It shows a woman holding a
leaf above her head, presumably from a
palm tree. A smaller statue of a Soviet
soldier once stood here too, but it was
taken away after the fall of Communism in
Hungary in 1989.

Jubilee Park (Jubileumi Park) is a good
place to get away from all the indoor
sightseeing of galleries and museums. It is
the perfect place to relax in the open air
under the shade of the trees, especially in
the heat of a summer afternoon. The park
was laid out on the south-facing slopes of
Gellért Hill in 1967 to mark the 50th
anniversary of the Russian Revolution –
hence the name Jubilee Park.

Flower beds and sweeping lawns are
interspersed with elegant statues, which
are a little less overpowering than the
bigger, bolder ones on the hill. The
children's area is popular for families
wanting to occupy their young ones for a
while.

The **Citadella** is a walled fort perched on
Castle Hill. It was built by the Habsburgs
in 1854 to keep control of this strategic
position overlooking the city. Over the
years it has had many uses, serving as a
military barracks, a prison and even a
refuge for German troops during the
Second World War. Now it caters more for
those passing through than those sent
here for incarceration of one sort or
another.

There is a hotel, a restaurant and a
casino, as well as various souvenir shops
selling trinkets. The views from the walls
are good, looking down over Budapest and
the Danube snaking past below.

The Citadella comes into its own each year
on St. Stephen's Day (August 20), when a
spectacular firework display is launched
from the battlements and rockets shower
down on the rooftops. This is probably the
one time of the year when it is best not to
be in the Citadella, for those down by the
river get the full benefit of the display.

Gellért Statue

XI. Gellérthegy
Ⓜ Ferenciek tere

Citadella

XI. Gellérthegy
Ⓜ Ferenciek tere
🕐 Mon-Sun: 8am-6pm.
Admission charge.

Cave Church

XI. Gellérthegy
Ⓜ Kálvin tér
☎ 385 1529
🕐 Mon-Sun: 8am-9pm.
Sun Mass: 11am & 5pm.

View from the Citadel

The **Cave Church** (Sziklatemplom), or Rock Chapel, is a place of worship carved out of the bu— of dolomite that makes up Castle Hill. It is administered by monks from the Paulite Order. Although one might expect this cave to be old, it actually dates from the 1920s.

The years from 1951 1961 were spent bricked up, courtesy of the communist regime, but it has enjoyed a steady stream of visitors since it was reopene— to the public in 1992. People come in to pray, give thanks or simply take a break.

The **Pál Molnár-C. Studio-Museum** (Molnár-C. Pál Muterem-Múzeum) is housed in the former home of this uniqu— artist and is run by his elderly daughter. Pál Molnár was a member of the Roman School of art and died in 1981. His surrealist style, often reminiscent of Dali's work, tackled both the sacred and the profane.

Pál Molnár-C. Studio-Museum

B

Ménesi út 65
☎ 361 1718
⏰ Nov-Mar: Tue-Thu: 3pm-6pm. Sun: 10am-1pm. Fri-Sat, Mon: closed. Apr-Oct: Tue-Thu: 3pm-6pm. Fri-Mon: closed
Admission charge.
2 admissions for the price of 1 with voucher on page 65.

Many of Buda's important attractions are found in the Castle District to the north c Gellért Hill and the Royal Palace. The tru— name of **Matthias Church** (Mátyás Templom) is the Church of Our Lady, bu— it was given its other title after King Matthias was married in it for the second time. He also added sections on to the original structure, which dates back to th— mid-13th century and the reign of Béla—

The outside is an interesting mix of tall windows, pinnacles and an elaborate 250 foot (76-metre) spire, added 600 years later but in keeping with the existing Gothic style. The menacing gargoyles tha— hang from the facade are hallmarks of th— architectural style.

The real treasures, however, lie inside. There are fine stained glass windows and

19th-century religious frescoes. The church is a leading venue for classical concerts, especially during the summer months.

The **Ecclesiastical Museum** spreads throughout various rooms, aisles and the crypt of the Matthias Church. There are collections of various religious artefacts and an imitation set of Hungary's crown jewels (the real ones glisten in the National Museum (page 31) and are well worth a visit). There is also a sarcophagus in this museum, which is said to contain the ancient bones from a royal tomb. (*Mátyás Templom, Ⓜ Batthyány tér, ☎ 355 5657. ⏲ Mon-Sun: 9am-7pm. Admission charge.*)

The **Golden Eagle Pharmaceutical Museum** is a small yet fascinating museum. It is a must for drug store owners everywhere, and anyone else with an eye for the unusual. This 15th-century house in the Castle Hill district near the Matthias Church provided the first pharmacy to serve the people of Buda.

The museum has only a few rooms but is an Aladdin's Cave of pharmaceutical memorabilia dating from the 16th and 17th centuries. The main attraction is a carefully laid out replica of a pharmacist's laboratory. The museum staff will explain the significance of the various bottles, bowls and boxes brimming with all sorts of bizarre pills and potions.

Mathias Church

Szentharomság tér 2
Ⓜ Batthyány tér
☎ 355 5657
⏲ Mon-Sun: 7am-7pm.

Golden Eagle Pharmaceutical Museum

Tarnok utca 18
Ⓜ Batthyány tér
☎ 317 9772
⏲ Tue-Sun: 10.30am-5.30pm. Mon: closed
Admission charge.

Matthias Church

Catacombs

Catacombs

Úri utca
Ⓜ Batthyány tér / Déli
station
☎ 212 0207/0287
🕓 Guided tours: Mar-
Oct: Mon-Sun: 9.30am-
7.30pm. Nov-Feb:
closed.
Admission charge.
**2 tours for the price of 1
with voucher on page
65. (Discounts on day
and evening basic tour
(Tour I) only).**

Under Castle Hill, a labyrinth of man-
made **Catacombs** link the caves cut by
ancient hot water springs. They served as
a refuge for prehistoric man half a million
years ago. More recently they have been
used as cellars, storerooms and baths.

In the 1930s, as part of the wartime
defence programme, they were converted
into a shelter to accommodate 10,000
people. Later, they were used as a secret
army bunker during the Cold War. Until
recently visitors had access to just one of
the 12 miles (19km) of passageways, but
in 1997 reconstruction work extended the
sightseeing area.

A walk through the labyrinth is a journey
through time, passing figures and scenes
from Hungarian history. The *Crowned
Head* represents the death of the
Hungarian king in the battle of Mohacs in
the 16th century and the subsequent
downfall of the independent Hungarian
kingdom at the hands of the Ottoman
armies. Another display recreates an
excavation revealing ancient cave
drawings.

The basic tour involves a commentary in
various languages, and night tours are
atmospherically lit with oil-lamps.

Longer tours incorporate drinks, a meal
and sometimes entertainment, which

involves music and dancing. You can even visit the mysterious **Personal Labyrinth**, which has been described as a place to 'search for the self'. It is open at night but an appointment is essential.

Another of Budapest's specialist museums, the **Telephone Museum** (Telefónia Múzeum) traces the history of telephony back to the late 19th century. The main reason for visiting this museum is to gain an understanding of communications heritage. It houses a rickety old telephone exchange that was used for 60 years up to 1985. This is an absorbing place for children to while away an hour or two playing with the exhibits and making phone calls to each other.

The dull name of the **Museum of Commerce and Catering** (Kereskedelmi és Vendéglátóipari Múzeum) is somewhat misleading. This museum houses snapshots of Budapest life that are well worth seeing, and is split into two exhibitions. In the commercial section there is a replica of a 19th-century grocer's shop complete with elaborate advertising signs (one is an early example of an electric sign). You can pick up a vintage poster replica from the shop.

There are also numerous examples of café society memorabilia from Budapest's old coffeehouses and hotels. The city once boasted hundreds of coffeehouses where people ate, danced and enjoyed live entertainment. The catering section covers everything a Budapest sweet shop and café owner would have needed to operate a roaring trade at the turn of the century.

Also known as the Museum of the History of Warfare, the **Museum of Military History** (Hadtörténeti Múzeum) is a must for anyone interested in soldiering and conflict and keen to learn about some of the rougher moments in Hungary's turbulent past.

There are exhibits chronicling the Turkish occupation of 1541, which lasted for 150 years until the United Christian armies finally drove them out. Sadly, much of the city was destroyed in the process. This display includes weapons, uniforms,

Telephone Museum

Úri utca 49
Ⓜ Batthyány tér / Déli station
☎ 212 2243
⊕ Apr-Sep: Tue-Sun: 10am-6pm. Nov-Mar: 10am-4pm. Mon: closed.
Admission charge.

Museum of Commerce and Catering

Fortuna utca 4
Ⓜ Batthyány tér
☎ 375 6249
⊕ Wed-Fri: 10am-5pm. Sat-Sun: 10am-6pm. Sat-Tue: closed.
Admission charge.

Fisherman's Bastion

medals and war maps.

There are also standards and weapons belonging to the commanders in the War of Independence (1848-9) and memorabilia from the First World War. More exciting and modern is the section dedicated to the 1956 revolution, or Hungarian Uprising, where there was hand-to-hand fighting in the streets.

The black-and-white photographic prints are striking and capture the imagination, putting the viewer right on the spot among the carnage and desperation. It is all laid out in a former barracks building dating from the 18th century and situated in the northwest sector of the Castle District. *(Tóth Árpad sétany 40, Ⓜ Moszkva tér, ☎ 356 8596. ⊕ Apr-Sep: Tue-Sun: 10am-6pm. Oct-Mar: Tue-Sun: 10am-4pm. Mon: closed. Admission charge and photo-permit charge.)*

Jewish Prayer House

Táncsics Mihály utca 26
Ⓜ Batthyány tér
☎ 342 1335
⊕ Tue-Fri: 10am-2pm.
Mon: closed. May-Oct:
Sat-Sun: 10am-6pm.
Nov-Apr: Sat-Sun:
closed.

Also known as the Small Synagogue, the **Jewish Prayer House** (Középkori Zsidó Imaház) is a Sephardic synagogue which dates back to the mid-1300s. It was built as a house of prayer by Jews returning to the Castle District from where they had been expelled a few years earlier. The vaulted ceiling previously carried Hebrew inscriptions in red paint.

Like many Hungarians, the nine Jewish communities of Budapest lived in fear of persecution because of the numerous sieges the city suffered. In the 17th century, the synagogue was converted into a house and its true purpose forgotten for

300 years until excavations in the 1960s unearthed it.

The **Museum of Music History** (Mta Zenetörténeti Múzeum) is one of two shrines in the city to one of Hungary's most famous composers, Béla Bartók (1881-1945). He spent much of his life collecting examples of Hungarian folk music, which influenced his own work.

The collection boasts a number of well-preserved instruments that date from the 17th, 18th and 19th centuries. There are violins, grand pianos, dulcimers, lyres, brass contraptions that look impossible to play, and other unusual folk instruments. There is even a set of bagpipes which were popular with folk musicians here.

One room is given over to the reconstruction of a Hungarian violin-maker's workshop, complete with tools, workbench and half-made instruments. Upstairs on the first floor is an archive containing hundreds of Bartók's manuscripts. It is believed Beethoven stayed in this house as a guest of the owner in 1800. Classical concerts are held here in the summer, but they are popular to book well in advance.

Fisherman's Bastion (Halászbástya), which looks rather like a Disneyland castle, offers one of the best viewpoints in town. From the fairytale turrets you can photograph a panorama of the Danube riverbank and Pest, including the Chain Bridge, Margaret Island and St. Stephen's Basilica.

Based on a former fortress wall, the bastion was actually designed and built between 1901 and 1902. It was named after the Danube fishermen whose job it was to defend the fish market that used to stand near here. The bastion is considered one of the must-see tourist attractions in Budapest. In the courtyard is a statue of St. Stephen, the first king of Hungary.

St. Anne's (Szent Anna templom) is considered to be one of the finest Baroque churches in the whole of Hungary. It was built in the second half of the 18th century. Its two ornate, domed towers rise up impressively from the entrance on Batthyány square.

Museum of Music History

Táncsics Mihály utca 7
Ⓜ Batthyány tér
☎ 214 6770
🕐 Mon: 4pm-8pm. Wed-Sun: 10am-6pm.
Tue: closed.
Admission charge.

Fisherman's Bastion

I. Várhegy
Ⓜ Batthyány tér
🕐 24 hours.
Admission charge for upper viewing gallery.

Just above the doorway there are stone sculptures representing Faith, Hope and Charity. Up above you can see St. Anne herself standing with the figure of Mary. The two appear together again as statues on the high altar. The ceiling of the church is graced with beautiful frescoes depicting the life of its saint. Delicate restoration work was necessary after the ceiling was badly damaged in the Second World War.

St. Anne's is a popular church, often bustling with people coming in to pray on their way to and from work. Nearby is the Angelika coffee house which presents a welcome break for tourists.

The **Foundry Museum** (Öntödei Múzeum) takes a look at Hungary's industrial past. Its metalwork and iron exhibits cover a large chunk of history from the Bronze Ag to the present day. It is located on the sit of an iron foundry built 150 years ago by the engineer Abraham Ganz.

The **Buda Hills** (Budai-hegység), are the attractive, leafy neighbourhoods where people come to walk in the fresh air. A map of the hills is a good idea if you are planning to walk off the beaten track. Th area is peppered with delightful parks an nature reserves and there are nature and pony-riding trails.

A unique way to travel there is the **Children's Railway** (Gyermek Vasút), a narrow-gauge route which is largely run b children. From **Moszkva Square**, one-way trips take a little less than an hour and a a lot of fun, with the young guards wearing little replica uniforms of the Hungarian National Railway staff. Alternatively, you can hop aboard the rather rickety but safe **János Chair Lift** (János Hegy Libego), which will whisk you to the top in minutes. This is the highest point in Budapest. On a clear day, you can see the Tatra mountains more than 100 miles (160km) away. In the winter this area is the domain of skiers and snowboarders. *(Children's Railway, ☎ 395 5420. ⊕ Mon-Fri: 10am-5pm. Sat-Sun: 10am-6pm. Sep-Mar: Mon: closed. Admission charge. János Chair Lift, ☎ 317 9800. ⊕ Apr-Sep: Mon-Sun: 9am-5pm. Nov-Mar: Mon-Sun 9am-4pm.)*

St. Anne's

Batthyány tér
Ⓜ Batthyány tér
☎ 201 6364
⊕ Services: Mon-Sat: 6.45am-9am, 4pm-7pm. Sun: 7am-1pm.

Foundry Museum

Bem József utca 20
Ⓜ Batthyány tér
☎ 202 5327
⊕ Mon-Sun: 9am-5pm. Admission charge.

Pest

The Pest riverbank of the Danube is dominated by one vast building – **Parliament (Országház)**. You have to join an organised tour, but it is well worth it for a look inside what was once the world's largest parliament building.

It was completed in 1904, after 19 years of construction. Its interior boasts 691 rooms and about 15 miles (24km) of staircase. The neo-Gothic style has been compared to the British Parliament building in London, although the central Neo-Renaissance dome is more reminiscent of St. Paul's Cathedral. The tip of the spire on top of the dome reaches a height of more than 90 metres (300 feet) above the ground.

Inside and directly below the dome lies a central hall where chamber music concerts are held in the summer. The price of a ticket usually includes a tour of the building.

During breaks in the political procedure, MPs meet in this atrium to relax, gossip and plot the downfall of their rivals. The cigar holders by the doors are reminders of the opulence attained by the privileged few.

This chamber is lined with the statues of former rulers of Hungary. On either side are waiting rooms, which lead to the chamber of the House of Representatives (where 386 currently sit) and the Congress

Parliament

Kossuth Lajos tér
Ⓜ Kossuth tér
☎ 268 4437
🕐 Tours: In session: Wed-Sun: 10am. In recess: Mon-Fri: 10am & 2pm. Sat: 10am & 12.30pm. Sun: 10am Admission charge. Concert tickets, ☎ 317 7031.

Parliament

St. Stephen's Basilica

Hall (formerly the Upper House, or Lords, which no longer exists).

There are statues of farm labourers, tradesmen and military men in the waiting rooms, each of which has its own colour-coded carpets – blue for the former Upper House and red for the Representatives.

The tour guide will explain the presence of the largest hand-made carpet in Europe which was painstakingly stitched together by peasants from a tiny village in the Hungarian countryside.

While the Parliament building has always boasted elegance, it was never known for democracy. Prior to the fall of Communism in 1989, there was only one brief sitting of a democratically elected government, between the end of the Second World War and the Communist takeover.

The **Museum of Ethnography** (Néprajzi Múzeum) is a treasure chest of heritage items that tell the story of the roots and the progression of Hungary's rural peoples.

The main permanent exhibition is entitled *The Traditional Culture of the Hungarian People* and includes costumes, examples of ancient rural folklore, and collections of everyday objects from across the country. There are helpful maps which reveal how many diverse cultures were present at the turn of the century and where they lived.

Guided tours are available in English, German, Italian, Spanish and Finnish for an extra charge. Alternatively, visitors can rent personal stereos with an hour-long commentary tape.

There are also several temporary exhibitions, concentrating on all things ethnographic, such as the history of gypsies in Hungary or the elaborate artwork produced by various ethnic groups. At certain times of the year, folk groups perform dances, plays and workshops here. The museum is situated in a grand, former government building.

The **Post Office Savings Bank** (Postatakarék) was completed in 1900 by the popular architect Odon Lechner. The ornamental designs he used derived chiefly from Hungarian folk culture. It is situated next to the National Bank and has been recently restored. The roof is alive with stone flowers and mythical beasts. Inside it is a working bank.

St. Stephen's Basilica (Szent István Bazilika), Budapest's biggest and most important church, has had a chequered history. Work first began in 1851 according to plans drawn up by the architect József Hild.

The dome fell in 17 years later and the entire building had to be razed and started again from scratch. There was more architectural heartache to come, when it became one of several buildings in Budapest damaged by Allied bombs in the Second World War. Workmen continue to fix it even today.

Most visitors drop in to the church to stare at one of Budapest's more gruesome exhibits. In a glistening shrine of silver and gold, shaped like a miniature church, see what are reputed to be the remains of the partially preserved right hand of St. Stephen. For a small fee, a light inside will flicker on, illuminating the relic to gasps from the crowd. Each year in August on St. Stephen's holy day the bones are carried through the streets of the city.

The church also holds less gory treasures, including some impressive examples of stained glass and a painting depicting St. Stephen presenting the crown of the Hungarian kings to the Virgin Mary. Most of the interior is the work of architect Miklos Ybl (who also built the Opera House). He and his team of artists worked

Museum of Ethnography

Kossuth Lajos tér 12
Ⓜ Kossuth tér
☎ 332 6340
🕑 Tue-Sun: 10am-6pm.
Mon: closed.
Admission charge.

Post Office Savings Bank

Hold utca 4
Ⓜ Árany János utca
☎ 311 4432
🕑 Thu: 9am-2pm.
Call to arrange tours
at other times.

on the building for much of the latter half of the 19th century. Outside, look for the heads of the 12 Apostles on the main gate and the Four Evangelists perched on the dome.

If you are nearby as a new hour is struck, take notice of the tolling of the bell. It was a gift from Germany in 1989, a generous way of righting the wrong done to St. Stephen's when German troops ran off with the original bell during the war.

St. Stephen's is a good place to catch chamber and choral concerts in the evenings, but ring in advance for tickets.

St. Stephen's Basilica

Szent István tér
Ⓜ Arany János utca / Bajcsy-Zsilinszky
☎ 317 2859
🕐 at time of Mass:
Mon-Sat: 9am-5pm.
Sun: 1pm-5pm.
Admission charge.
2 admissions for the price of 1 with voucher on pages 65.

Gresham Palace was never actually a palace but an office building for an English insurance company. Nevertheless it was designed with grandeur in mind. It is considered by some to be the city's best known and most popular Art Nouveau building and was acclaimed when it opened in 1907. Though badly in need of a refit, its future looks promising since it i planned to become a hotel.

There is a glass-covered tunnel that visitors can walk through. The insurance clerks have long gone, and have been replaced by a restaurant, a casino and several small shops. The best time to view and photograph the palace is as the sun i sinking, when the last rays of the day catch the gilded tiles on the roof, making them shine.

Gresham Palace

Roosevelt tér 5
Ⓜ Vörösmarty tér
☎ 267 3745

The **Post Office Museum** (Posta Múzeum) gives a brief history lesson on the Hungarian Postal Service. The main exhibit is a replica of a working post office, and there is also a collection of postal vans. Look out for the pretty frescoes in the hallway which were painte by Károly Lotz, who was also responsible for much of the interior decor of the Opera House. *(Andrássy út 3, Ⓜ Bajcsy Zsilinszky út, ☎ 269 6838. 🕐 Apr-Oct: Tue-Sun 10am-6pm. Nov-Mar: 10am-4pm. Mon: closed Admission charge.)*

The **Underground Railway Museum** (Földalatti Múzeum) comprises a collectio of old underground train carriages lined up along a disused platform in the Deák Ferenc tér station. They are significant because Budapest's was the first electric underground railway in Europe and became a model for the rest of the continent's metro systems.

The carriages have been quite well preserved. It is fun to peer through the windows and imagine what commuting must have been like on the wooden seats of one of these bone-shakers in 1896, when the first ones rattled through the tunnels under the streets. They also give off the unmistakeable smell shared by all subterranean railways the world over – a mixture of earth, wood and brake dust.

Designed and built between 1875 and 1884 by the architect Miklós Ybl (who was working on St. Stephen's Basilica at about the same time), the **Opera House** (Operaház) is truly magnificent. It is high on the list of Europe's top opera venues. It is renowned for its acoustics, and has a hectic performance programme which puts rival houses to shame.

It has recently enjoyed a major refurbishment that has left it sparkling. By the three-arched entrance are statues of Franz Liszt (who was instrumental in establishing the Budapest Academy of Music) and Ferenc Erkel (who was the Opera's first director). He was followed later by the composer Gustav Mahler.

The first things to strike visitors as they pass into the entrance hall are the gilded ceiling, mosaic floor and handsome white

Underground Railway Museum

Deák Ferenc tér
Ⓜ Deák tér
☎ 461 6500
🕑 Tue–Sun: 10am–6pm. Mon: closed.
Admission charge.

Gresham Palace

Interior of the Opera House

marble staircase. The auditorium is adorned with gold and is built with three levels of balconies overlooking the stalls. A vast bronze chandelier, weighing more than two tonnes, hangs from among the Greek gods, and an orchestra of angels is painted on the frescoed ceiling.

If you can get into the corridor of the performers' entrance you will see the walls are covered with the sketched busts of a gallery of opera greats. Not all of the 1,261 seats are filled every night, so last-minute tickets can often be bought.

At the **National Lutheran Museum** (Evangélikus Múzeum) most exhibits tell the story of the Hungarian Evangelical Church, but there is also a copy of Martin Luther's will.

The original is in the church next door. Guided tours can be arranged with some of the former clergy who worked and worshipped here. The church itself is fairly stark and parts of it are only open during services. One of the best ways to see it is by coming to a concert here, as it plays host to a lively programme of musical events.

Also known as the Dohany Temple, the **Central Synagogue** (Nagy Zsinagóga) is the largest synagogue in Europe and second only to the Temple Emmanuel in New York. It can hold 3,000 people – men in

Opera House

Magyar Állami Operaház

Andrássy út 22
Ⓜ Opera
☎ 332 8197
⏲ Guided tours (English): Mon-Sun: 3pm and 4pm.
Admission charge.
2 tours for the price of 1 with voucher on page 65.

the stalls, women in the dress circle.

It was completed in 1859 by the architect Ludwig Förster, who had previously gained fame for building a synagogue in Vienna. His style is described as Moorish because it draws on some of the ideas of Islamic architecture. He used cast iron and natural coloured bricks in his design.

The facade of the building is framed by two towers, both containing staircases and topped with domes measuring 130 feet (40 metres) in height. The wide entrance hall leads into a huge temple, which is surrounded on three sides by galleries.

The interior was designed by Frigyes Feszl. The pulpit is one of the most beautiful to be found in any religious monument in the city. The Torah-Ark is of such proportions that it looks like a small temple inside this much bigger one.

The synagogue has been a working centre of religious study for several rabbis, but it is also a place of pilgrimage.

Cantor competitions and organ recitals attract large crowds. A **Holocaust Memorial** (a metal weeping willow inscribed with the names of those who lost their lives) stands in the courtyard and should not be missed.

The **Jewish Museum** (Zsidó Múzeum), built by architects Laszló Vágó and Ference Faragó, opened in 1931 behind the Central Synagogue. Exhibitions are housed on two floors. Note the windows of stained glass depicting Jewish religious scenes. One memorable exhibition, created to commemorate the Emancipation in 1938, survived unscathed through the Second World War hidden in the basement of the Hungarian National Museum.

The building played a key role in the war. In 1944 it served as a secret passageway through which people earmarked for deportation could escape from the confines of the ghetto.

Permanent exhibits include objects associated with Jewish holidays and rituals, the mementos of Jewish life, and documents dating from the period of

National Lutheran Church and Museum

Deák Ferenc tér 4
Ⓜ Deák ter
☎ 317 4173
🕐 Tue-Sun: 10am-6pm.
Mon: closed.
Admission charge.

Central Synagogue

Dohány utca 2
Ⓜ Astoria
☎ 342 8949
🕐 Mon-Fri: 10am-3pm.
Sun: 10am-1pm.
Sat: closed.
Admission charge.

serious anti-semitism earlier this century.

A church has stood on the site of the **Inner City Parish Church** (Belvárosi Plébánia) for almost a thousand years. The present structure is an amalgamation of hundreds of years of religious architectural styles. It is worth joining the Latin Mass on a Sunday morning just for the experience. *(Március 15 tér, Ⓜ Ferenciek tére, ☎ 318 3108. ⏱ Mon-Sat: 6am-7pm. Sun: 8am-7pm. Mass: Sun: 10am. Admission is free.)*

Jewish Museum

Dohány utca 2
Ⓜ Astoria
☎ 342 8949
⏱ Mon-Fri: 10am-3pm.
Sun: 10am-1pm.
Sat: closed.
Admission charge.

There are numerous contemporary art galleries dotted around the city specialising in everything from drawings to Pop art, photography and design. The **Budapest Gallery Exhibition Space** (Galéria Kiállítóterem) shows a selection of each of these, as well as token examples of architecture. The gallery also oversees displays at the **Exhibition House** (Kiállítóháza) which is situated at Lajos utca 158 *(☎ 388 6771).*

Perfect for children, **Károlyi Gardens** (Károlyi kert) is one of the better playgrounds in Budapest. The dog ban (enforced by means of a fence around the perimeter) means the area is remarkably clean. It is a pleasant place to take a break from the round of cultural visits and pass a leisurely hour or two in the middle of a busy tour schedule.

Lovers of Hungarian literature should head

Central Synagogue

for the **Hungarian Museum of Literature** (Petőfi Irodalmi Múzeum) in the Neo-Classical **Károlyi Palace** (Károlyi Palota). The displays are predominantly in Hungarian, and there are a number of permanent and temporary exhibits examining Hungarian writers and their work.

The museum is named after

Sándor Petőfi, a radical poet remembered
for reading aloud his poem 'National Song'
on the steps of the National Museum on
March 15 1848. He rallied people to
follow him in a revolution against the rule
of the Habsburgs. The event is still
celebrated each year with a show of
national pride.

The Károlyi Palace and Gardens are
named after Mihály Károlyi. In 1918 he
became the first president of the
Hungarian Republic and lived in the
palace during his rule. Until recently, one
of the rooms was devoted to the man
himself as an annexe to the main
museum. However, it was removed in
1990 for political reasons.

Mesegaléria is an art gallery for children. It
displays sketches and paintings from
Hungary's traditional children's literature.
The names of the illustrators may not be
familiar to non-Hungarians, but many of
the works are delightful and copies are for
sale. Adults may have to bend down a
little to examine the pieces, which are
hung low so that young children can
admire them.

The **Hungarian National Museum** (Magyar
Nemzeti Múzeum) is the oldest museum
in the city and was completed in 1847.
The collections inside are divided into
archaeology, the history of the people and
royal insignia.

The archaeology rooms cover Hungary's
history from the Stone Age to the Middle
Ages. Among the many interesting exhibits
are a Roman mosaic floor dating from the
3rd century BC. There are also displays of
jewellery, weapons and ornaments.

There is a room devoted to the War of
Independence in 1848. This is particularly
appropriate because the rebels who
quelled the revolution against the
Habsburgs, led by the poet Sandor Petőfi,
met on the museum's steps and rallied
local people to follow them. Petőfi's brave
plan worked and March 15 1848 – the
day when he read to the people his ode to
freedom, 'National Song' – is
commemorated each year. The show of
nationalism at the museum involves
speeches and much waving of the

Budapest Gallery Exhibition Space

Szabadsajtó út 5
Ⓜ Ferenciek tere
☎ 318 8097
🕐 Tue-Sun: 10am-6pm.
Mon: closed.
Admission charge.

Museum of Hungarian Literature

Károlyi Mihály utca 16
Ⓜ Ferenciek tere
☎ 317 3611
🕐 Apr-May: Tue-Sun:
10am-6pm.
Nov-Mar: Tue-Sun:
10am-4pm. Mon: closed.
Admission charge.

Mesegaléria

Besci Utca 3
Ⓜ Vörösmarty tér
☎ 317 7843
🕐 Tue-Sat: 10am-6pm.
Sun-Mon: closed.

Hungarian National Museum

Hungarian flag.

Another room contains the tent of a Turkish army leader and a third the royal regalia, where the Holy Crown, or St. Stephen's Crown, is found. It has only been on display here for the past 20 years since being returned from America, where it was stored for safe keeping after the Second World War. The name, however, is a bit misleading because the crown does not actually date back as far as St. Stephen, who reigned between 1000 and 1038. In fact, it appears to be made up of ornaments from a number of later periods. Regardless of its heritage, it is beautiful to look at and is encrusted with pearls and precious stones.

There are also more modern displays recounting life in Hungary in the First World War and the days of dictatorship. For nature lovers, the museum contains a Natural History Department situated in the south wing.

Budapest is blessed with several grand markets. These are always a hive of activity and are ideal for photographers (and, sadly, pickpockets). One of the biggest is the **Central Market Hall** (Központi Vásárcsarnok), which bustles with stall-holders and shoppers alike and is now a protected building. When the hall was first built roughly 100 years ago, provision was made for canal barges to glide right inside and drop off their cargo.

The **Bible Museum** (Biblia Múzeum) holds the priceless Ráday Collection, which belongs to the Danubian Diocese of the Reformed Church. There are several valuable old bibles on display here, including one from Germany dating from 1599 and a Hebrew bible from Basle in Switzerland that is about 70 years older

Hungarian National Museum

Múzeum körút 14-16
Ⓜ Kálvin tér
☎ 338 2122
🕐 Apr-Oct: Tue-Sun: 10am-6pm. Nov-Mar: Tue-Sun: 10am-5pm. Mon: closed.
Guided tours available.
Admission charge.

than that. Others of a lesser age and in obscure tribal languages are also exhibited here. *(Ráday utca 28, Ⓜ Ferenc körut, ☎ 217 6321. ◷ Tue-Sun: 10am-5pm. Mon: closed. Free admission.)*

The **Museum of Applied Arts** (Iparművészeti Múzeum) was inspired by London's South Kensington museums. It was founded in 1872 with the intention of providing a platform for art objects and furnishings.

Its permanent exhibition is devoted to Arts and Crafts, displaying materials and charting the changes in the techniques and technology of decorative handcrafts. The exhibition *Style 1900 – A Great Experiment in Modernism in the Applied Arts* displays some 700 works and recalls the sparkling lifestyles of the turn of the century and the richness of the artistic forms of this time. The location, one of the finest buildings of the Art Nouveau era, itself contributes to the impact of the display.

There are always temporary exhibits covering a variety of fields, from furniture, textiles, crystal and glassware to fine ceramics and jewellery.

Budapest is very proud of its new **Natural History Museum** (Természettudományi Múzeum). It opened in 1996 in what was once the Ludovika Military Academy.

The main permanent exhibit, 'Man and

Central Market Hall

Vámház körút 1-3
☎ 217 6067
Ⓜ Kálvin tér
◷ Mon: 6am-5pm. Tue-Fri: 6am-6pm. Sat: 6am-2pm. Sun: closed.

for less **Museum of Applied Arts**

Üllői út 33-37
Ⓜ Ferenc Körút
☎ 217 5222
◷ Mar 12-Dec 13: Tue-Sun: 10am-6pm. Dec 14-Mar 11: Tue-Sun: 10am-4pm. Mon: closed. Admission and photography permit charge.
2 admissions for the price of 1 with voucher on page 67.

Museum of Applied Arts

Nature in Hungary', examines the relationship between humans and the natural world, and looks at how one has affected the other.

Another exhibit, 'Flowers That Never Fade', displays a selection of treasures from the museum's minerals collection. There is also a collection of stones and fossils from around the country.

The Discovery Room is full of fun, interactive exhibits. Objects that can be handled include an elephant skull and a stuffed brown bear.

There is a model of a prehistoric cave complete with a life-size replica of a woolly mammoth, an animal that once roamed Hungary in large herds.

There are frequent temporary exhibits, which in the past have covered a wide range of natural history topics, including trees, hunting, the Frozen World and Hungarian Insects.

Natural History Museum

Ludovika tér 6
Ⓜ Nagyvárad tér
☎ 313 0842
🕑 Wed–Mon: 10am–5pm (later in summer).
Tue: closed.
Admission charge.
2 admissions for the price of 1 with voucher on page 67.

Visitors to the **Kerepesi Cemetery** (Kerepesi Temető) will find the graves of some of Hungary's most influential figures. Notable political tombs include those of Lajos Batthyány, who was prime minister of the independent government of 1848; Ferenc Deák, who brokered the Compromise with Austria in 1867; and József Antall, who was the first Prime Minister to take the helm after the fall of Communism in 1990.

Natural History Museum

As for heroes, there is the tomb of revolutionary Lajos Kossuth, a lawyer who demanded complete independence from Austria and the abolition of the feudal system that enslaved the peasants. He led the revolution against the Habsburgs.

The arts are represented by a variety of singers, writers and poets. The tree-lined avenues between the tombs are pleasant to walk down.

The **Stamp Museum** (Bélyeg Múzeum) is a giant collection of stamps from across the world, including every stamp issued in Hungary in the past 120 years. Many of the ones bearing the name Magyar Posta are elaborately designed and printed. Some are oversized, while others are triangular in shape.

The museum is a treat for philatelists, with a collection so huge that the actual number of items within it can only be estimated. *(Hársfa utca 47,* Ⓜ *Blaha Lujza tér,* ☎ *341 5526.* ◷ *Apr-Oct: Tue-Sun: 10am-6pm. Nov-Mar: Tue-Sun: 10am-4pm. Mon: closed. Admission charge.)*

The **Franz Liszt Museum** (Liszt Ferenc Múzeum) is located in the house in which the famous Hungarian pianist and composer spent his last few years, before his death in 1886. The museum is well laid out and is an authentic reconstruction of what life would have been like here over 100 years ago. The furniture Liszt used is all in place, along with a number of his possessions.

With Berlioz, Liszt was considered to be one of the chief musical proponents of the romantic era in the 19th century. Look out for the various instruments, mainly pianos, in the collection, and the mobile keyboard that he carried with him to play and compose.

Concerts are performed on Saturday mornings and there is a research centre for students of the great man and his music.

The **Puppet Theatre** (Bábszinház) is professional puppeteering at its best. The characters come mainly from fairy tales and there are more than a few romantic castles on craggy hilltops where hungry

Kerepesi Cemetery

Fiumei út 16
Ⓜ Keleti pu.
☎ 333 9125
◷ Mon-Sun: 7am-8pm (earlier in winter).

Franz Liszt Museum

Vörösmarty utca 35
Ⓜ Vörösmarty utca
☎ 322 9804
◷ Mon-Fri: 10am-6pm.
Sat: 9am-5pm.
Sun and 1st three weeks of Aug: closed.
Admission charge.
2 tours for the price of 1 with voucher on page 67.

Heroes' Square

wolves roam and threaten damsels. There are two puppet theatres that are open from September through the winter months and up to the middle of June. *(Budapesti Bábszinház at Andrássy út 69,* Ⓜ *Vörösmarty utca,* ☎ *321 5200. Kolibri szinház a Jókai tér 10,* Ⓜ *Oktogon,* ☎ *353 4633.* ⊕ *Call ahead for times of shows and admission charges.)*

Kodaly Memorial Museum

Andrássy út 87-89
Ⓜ Kodály körönd
☎ 342 8448
⊕ Wed: 10am-4pm.
Thu-Sat: 10am-6pm.
Sun: 10am-2pm.
Mon-Tue: closed.
Admission charge.
2 admissions for the price of 1 with voucher on page 67.

The **Kodály Memorial Museum** (Kodály Emlék Múzeum) is the house where the noted composer and musicologist lived and worked for more than 40 years. He died here in 1967 at the age of 85.

Zoltán Kodály, like his fellow Hungarian and great friend Béla Bartók, endlessly scoured the countryside for traditional arrangements of folk tunes and gypsy songs. He also found international fame for developing a unique way to teach children using music.

The house comprises a library, sitting room and dining room, which are all in much the same order as when he died. Also on display are some original manuscripts of his work. Kodály has been immortalised in bronze by the sculptor Imre Varga, whose statue of him stands on Castle Hill (page 10).

The collection of the **Ferenc Hopp Museum of Eastern Asiatic Arts** (Kelet-Ázsia Művészeti Múzeum) contains many politically, culturally and spiritually significant pieces of East Asian antiquity.

Sculptures, carpets, jewellery, painted scrolls and numerous other artworks are all present, the fruits of Hopp's frequent travels to Asia in the 18th century. Over the years he amassed the thousands of interesting items that make up this impressive collection. Although it was once housed in its own museum, it was recently combined with and moved to the **György Ráth Museum** (formerly the other major collection of East Asian antiquities in Budapest). György Ráth was an artist as well as an art historian and collector. His collection included more everyday items, like bottles and vanity equipment, but there are also paintings, scrolls and shrines. This enlarged museum is a must for those interested in Asiatic art.

György Ráth Museum

Városligeti fasor 12
Ⓜ Bajza utca
☎ 342 3916
🕑 Apr-Oct: Tue-Sun: 10am-6pm. Nov-Mar: Tue-Sun: 10am-5pm. Mon: closed.
Admission charge.

The Millennary Monument and Archangel Gabriel statue stand at one end of **Heroes' Square** (Hősök tere). The Tomb of the Unknown Soldier is nearby and all around are the ghosts of Hungary's past, reliving the many events that have happened here. The square is very popular with Budapest's skateboarding youth.

The **Museum of Fine Arts** (Szépművészeti Múzeum) celebrated its ninetieth birthday in 1996. Its establishment marked the anniversary of the first millennium of the Hungarian nation. Designed by architects Albert Schickedanz and Fulop Herzog, it was opened in 1906. Originally, the upper floor of the Neo-Classical building was devoted to paintings, while the ground floor displayed plaster casts of some of the great sculptures of the world. As the museum acquired more original sculptures these imitations were replaced. Only one copy remains, the *Temple of Zeus at Olympia* on the facade of the building.

Tomb of the Unknown Soldier

Museum of Fine Arts

Museum of Fine Arts

for less

Hősök tere
M Hősök tere
☎ 343 9759
🕙 Tue–Sun: 10am–
5.30pm. Mon: closed.
Admission charge.
2 admissions for the
price of one with
voucher on page 67.

Kunsthalle

for less

IV. Dózsa Gyögy út 37
M Hősök tere
☎ 343 7401
🕙 Tue–Sun: 10am–6pm.
Mon: closed.
Admission charge.
2 admissions for the
price of one with
voucher on pages 67.

The Old Masters Gallery has nearly 3,000 European paintings from the 13th to the 18th centuries, the most impressive coming from Spain. The fine prints and drawings of famous painters and sculptures are often displayed in temporary exhibitions.

The ground floor houses classical antiquities, 19th-century paintings and sculptures, renaissance frescoes and temporary graphic art exhibits. A new level has recently opened containing the Egyptian Collection and 20th-century artworks. Guided tours in English are available but must be booked in advance.

Opposite stands the **Kunsthalle** (Műcsarnok), the largest of its kind in the country. It was the creation of Schickedanz and Herzog, who designed the Museum of Fine Arts, and the two Greek Revival buildings complement each other across the square. Its splendid renaissance facade features a mosaic of St. Stephen which was added in 1941.

Since its inauguration in 1896, the Exhibition Hall has displayed temporary collections of art and sculpture by both Hungarian and foreign artists, except during the First World War when it functioned as a military hospital. It also holds lectures, film shows and children's workshops.

City Park (Városliget) is a great spot in which to walk and relax. The park extends over roughly one square mile right in the centre of the city. There is a boating lake that doubles as an ice rink in winter, and the **Budapest Zoo** (below) is found here.

Tourists also come to the park to visit **Castle Vajdahunyad** (Vajdahunyad vara), a replica of a Romanian fortress. Sitting on an island in the lake, it was built to commemorate the 1,000th year of the nation in 1896. It is most impressive when lit up at night, its reflected lights dancing in the water. The castle now houses the **Museum of Agriculture** (page 40).

Other attractions in the City Park include an amusement park, an open-air theatre, the **Széchenyi Baths**, the **Millenary Monument**, an art gallery, the **Municipal Grand Circus**, the **Transport Museum** and the **Museum of Fine Arts** (page 37). There are also several playgrounds and recreation areas, including a garden for the blind planted with strong-smelling plants. (*Dózsa György út,* Ⓜ *Hősök tere / Széchenyi Gyógyfürdő. Free admission to park.*)

The **Budapest Zoo** (Állatkert) is one of the oldest zoos in the world, opening in 1866. Thankfully, the facilities have been updated to reflect today's more humane practises.

Today it has approximately 500 animal species and 4,000 plant types, and is an important centre of nature conservation. It claims that over one million visitors pass through its gates each year.

The palm house is the country's largest tropical greenhouse. There is a breeding programme for endangered animals of the Danube Basin. As

Budapest Zoo

Állatkerti körút 6-12
Ⓜ Széchenyi fürdő
☎ 343 6075
🕐 All year: Mon–Sun: 9am–dusk. Last admission one hour before closing. Admission charge.
2 admissions for the price of 1 with voucher on page 69.

Castle Vajdahunyad

well as the usual zoo animals, which include elephants, big cats and remarkable collections of primates and invertebrates, there is a section devoted to traditional Hungarian livestock, set in the reconstruction of a peasant farm with period buildings.

The zoo is also noted for the innovative architecture of its enclosures. Neuschloss' Art Nouveau elephant house and the traditionally Hungarian-style buildings designed by Károly Kós are particularly notable. The exhibits are labelled in English as well as in Hungarian.

Agriculture Museum

Vajdahunyad Castle,
Városliget
Ⓜ Hősök tere
☎ 343 0573
🕐 Mar–Nov: Tue–Fri and
Sun: 10am–5pm. Sat:
10am–6pm. Dec–Feb:
Tue–Fri: 10am–4pm.
Sat–Sun: 10am–5pm.
Mon: closed.
Admission charge.

Situated in the striking Vajdahunyad Castle, the **Museum of Agriculture** (Mezőgazdasági Múzeum) charts the history of Hungary's farming industry and shows how the rural population has suffered over the years.

The permanent exhibitions run through the history of animal husbandry and crop growing, and also demonstrate how the country developed its forestry, hunting and fishing industries. Temporary exhibitions in the past have covered such topics as the emancipation of the serfs and its effect on peasant culture.

The castle itself is well worth a wander around, or you could go for a walk by the lake side.

Whatever the ailment, the hot springs at **Széchényi Baths** (Széchényi Gyógyfürdő)

A lion cub at the zoo

are sure to help. This is one of the biggest spa complexes in Europe, and the waters are known across the continent for their restorative properties. Visitors can swim in the pools, take some exercise, relax in the sauna and even play chess on waterproof boards. *(Állatkerti körút 11, Ⓜ Széchenyi Gyógyfürdő, ☎ 321 0310. ☺ May-Sep: Mon-Sun: 6am-7pm. Oct-Mar: Mon-Fri: 6am-7pm. Sat-Sun: 6am-5pm. Admission charge.)*

Transport Museum

Every conceivable mode of transport is represented at the **Transport Museum** (Közlekedési Múzeum). The permanent exhibitions include 'A Century of Motor Transportation in Hungary', '150 years of Hungarian Railways', 'A Century of Hungarian State Shipping', 'The History of Road Transportation', 'The History of Urban Transportation' and 'Aviation and Space Flight'. One of the most interesting topics is the development of Budapest's metro, which dates from 1896 and was the first of its kind in Europe.

There is an aeronautical section with models of various flying machines. Visitors can get close to some old cars, steam engines and trams, but the rest of the exhibits are on a read-only basis and are nearly all in Hungarian, although the railway exhibition has information in English and German. English language tours can be arranged but must be booked in advance.

Városligeti körút 11
Ⓜ Mexikói út
☎ 343 0565/63
☺ Oct-Apr: Tue-Fri:
10am-4pm. Sat-Sun:
10am-5pm. May-Sep:
Tue-Fri: 10am-5pm.
Sat-Sun: 10am-6pm.
Mon: closed.
Admission charge.
2 admissions for the price of 1 with voucher on page 69.

The **Palace of Wonders** (Csodák Palotája) is aptly named. It is an informative and fun hands-on science museum, conceived specifically with children in mind, though popular with adults too.

It opened in 1997 and is considered an impressive step forward for Budapest tourism. There are entertaining, yet practical, user-friendly demonstrations of scientific phenomena, such as how a laser works, and numerous optical illusions to baffle the brain.

Almost all the exhibits are interactive. Visitors choose what buttons to press and knobs to turn, and can then watch the results of their actions. Two of the most popular exhibits are the 'Magic Flying Carpet' and the 'Disobedient Shadow'.

Palace of Wonders

Váci út 19
Ⓜ Lehel tér
☎ 350 6397
☺ Tue-Fri: 9am-5pm.
Sat-Sun: 10am-6pm.
Mon: closed.
Admission charge.
2 admissions for the price of 1 with voucher on page 69.

Óbuda and the North

The Danube at night

Margaret Island (Margitsziget) is a naturally-occurring island in the Danube stretching between the Árpád and Margit bridges, the latter of which kinks in the middle. Both a princess and a saint, Margaret was the daughter of King Béla IV. She established a convent on the island near to a church – the ruins of both can be visited today.

Margaret Island

Ⓜ Nyugati tér

Private cars are banned on Margaret Island and alternative modes of transport – bicycles, horse-drawn carriages and walking – are vigorously encouraged. It has made this river island in the centre of the city a good place to relax.

There are several public swimming pools. The **Palatinus Strand** is an elaborate water complex comprising seven pools, one of them warmed by thermal hot springs, as well as water slides and a wave machine. The Thermal Hotel boasts three pools, which are kept at toe-curling temperatures by jets of hot water bubbling up from springs in the rock beneath its foundations. *(Thermal Hotel, Ⓜ Margit hid, ☎ 329 2300. Palatinus Strand, Ⓜ Margit hid, ☎ 340 4505. ⊕ Opening hours vary.)*

Other sights include the 12th-century chapel dedicated to **St. Michael**, a zoo, a rose garden, a fountain erected in 1972 to mark the centenary of the union of Buda,

Pest and Óbuda, and an open-air theatre where opera is frequently performed. There is also an area given over to sculptures of Hungary's most famous artists, musicians and writers.

Óbuda means Old Buda and is, as you would expect, the oldest part of the city. The Romans liked the spot so much they settled here, calling the place **Aquincum**. It soon became the capital of a province of their empire which was known as Pannonia. The ruins include the remains of some Roman Baths and an amphitheatre (near Flórián tér and the railway station). Almost certainly the major reason why the Romans were attracted to this area was because of the hot springs.

Also nearby are the remains of a villa believed to have belonged to a Roman of some standing, an official possibly connected to the garrison situated by the river where the Árpád Bridge now stands.

Visitors are recommended to use a detailed map of the area to locate the various exhibits, which can be hard to find among the confusion of roads. Call venues in advance because some of them seem to have sporadic opening hours. *(Aquincum Museum and Roman Town (Aquincumi Múzeum), Szentendrei út 139, ☎ 368 8241/250 1650. ⊕ May-Sep: Tue-Sun: 9am-6pm. Apr 15-30 and Oct: Tue-Sun: 9am-5pm. Mon and Nov-Apr 14: closed. Admission charge. 2 admissions for the price of 1 with voucher on page 69.)*

Gul Baba's Tomb

Mecset utca 14
⊕ Tue-Sun: 10am-4pm.
Mon: closed.
Admission charge.

Gul Baba was a Turkish holy man whose name translates as the Father of the Flowers or Father of the Roses. He died here in 1541, the same year the Turks invaded and began their 150-year rule over the city. **Gul Baba's Tomb** is situated in a neighbourhood known, appropriately, as the Hill of Roses (Rózsadomb).

The **Óbuda Exhibit** (Óbudai Múzeum) is a small but interesting museum. It traces the history of this oldest section of Budapest through photographs and collections of everyday objects.

It is housed in one section of the Zichy Mansion (Zichy Kastely), the home of the Zichy family which was built in 1775. It also contains memorial rooms to the poet and painter Lajos Kassak. *(Fő tér 1, ☎ 250 1020. Tue-Fri: 2pm-6pm. Sat-Sun: 10am-6pm. Mon: closed. Admission charge.)*

The **Imre Varga Collection** (Varga Imre Gyűjtemény) is devoted to the popular, contemporary sculptor whose work is regarded as both beautiful and harrowing. Visitors might have already seen his work around Budapest.

One of his most famous pieces is a statue of Imre Nagy, the Prime Minister following the Hungarian Uprising in 1956 who was subsequently executed when the Soviet troops marched into the city, which stands near the Houses of Parliament (page 23). Another is the Holocaust Memorial (page 29), a metallic weeping willow with the names of victims inscribed on the leaves, which was erected outside the Central Synagogue in 1990. *(Laktanya utca 7, ☎ 250 0274. ⊕ Tue-Sun: 10am-6pm. Mon: closed. Admission charge.)*

The **Victor Vasarely Museum** (Vasarely Múzeum) is a spacious gallery showing as many as 400 of the artist's works. One of the founders of the Op Art movement, he was born in the southern Hungarian town of Pecs. When the country fell into chaos in 1919, he fled and sought exile in France. He died in 1997 at the age of 89. *(Szentlélek tér 6, ☎ 250 1540. ⊕ Tue-Sun: 10am-6pm. Admission charge.)*

Zsigmund Kun spent years travelling around the countryside collecting things of interest, from pots and pans to ornate chairs and tables. The **Zsigmund Kun Folk Art Collection** (Kun Zsigmund Népművészeti Gyújtemény) displays these items and gives the visitor a snapshot of rural life over the last 200 years. *(Fő tér 4, ☎ 250 1020. ⊕ Tue-Fri: 2pm-6pm. Sat-Sun 10am-6pm. Mon: closed. Admission charge.)*

Béla Bartók was obsessed with folk tradition in the rural areas of Hungary and spent much time visiting farmsteads and gathering folk tunes that later heavily influenced his music. The **Béla Bartók Memorial House** (Bartók Béla Emlékház) in the family home, contains photographs and personal letters to Bartók. Concerts are held here some evenings.

Béla Bartók Memorial House

Csalán út 29
☎ 394 2100
⊕ Tue-Sun: 10am-5pm.
Mon: closed.
Admission charge.

Kiscelli Museum

Kiscelli utca 108
☎ 388 8560
⊕ Apr-Oct: Tue-Sun: 10am-6pm. Nov-Mar: Tue-Sun: 10am-4pm.
Mon: closed.
Admission charge.
2 admissions for the price of 1 with voucher on page 69.

The **Kiscelli Múzeum** is devoted to Hungarian art and culture. On display are artworks from the past 100 years, many of which have clearly been influenced by popular western European schools of art. Impressionism, Cubism and Surrealism are all represented in the brush strokes. There are also engravings and statues, an interesting collection of Hungarian newspapers charting the ups and downs of the country, and a working printing press. Another part of the museum has objects that reflect everyday life in the city since the Middle Ages.

It is worth a short excursion into the hilly neighbourhoods of Pálvölgyi and Zoldmal in District II just for the tours into the **Szelmő-hegy and Pálvölgyi Caves** (Szelmő-hegy and Pálvölgyi barlang). They are a rare phenomenon, hollowed out of the rock by the minerals in the hot springs bubbling up from the earth's crust, rather than from rainwater trickling down through the ground, as with most cave formations. Pálvölgy is famous for its stalactites that hang down like giant rock icicles. While not particularly long, the walk through the cave can be tiring as there are hundreds of steps to climb.

The two caves are a short walk from each other and a 20-minute stroll from the river and Margaret Island. They offer a cool break from the summer heat.

Szelmő-hegy and Pálvölgyi Caves

Szelmő-hegy barlang
Pusztaszeri út 35
☎ 325 6001
🕐 Wed-Fri and Mon:
10am-3pm. Sat-Sun:
10am-4pm. Tue: closed.
Admission charge.
**2 admissions for the
price of 1 with voucher
on page 69.**

Pálvölgyi barlang
Szépvölgyi út 162
☎ 325 9505
🕐 Tue-Sun: 10am-4pm.
Mon: closed.
Admission charge.
**2 admissions for the
price of 1 with voucher
on page 71.**

Pálvölgyi Caves

Beyond the City

The charming town of **Szentendre** lies an hour-and-a-half boat ride (even less by car or train) north of Budapest, in an area known locally as the Danube Bend. It is well worth a day trip.

Settled by Serbians as they fled the invading Turkish armies in the 14th century, and their influence remains today, most strikingly in the town's beautiful Serbian churches.

Szentendre is very crowded in the summer when the triangular, main market square and nearby streets fill up with stalls selling curios to tourists, but you can still get away from it all down the back streets. If you are lucky you might bump into one of the scores of artists who live here and form part of a colony.

The artists' colony was established at the turn of the century and has spawned a myriad of museums and galleries, many of which are open to the public. Almost all the works on display are modern, many of them having been painted since the Second World War. Some are for sale.

A Hungarian woman in country dress

For information once in Szentendre visit the **JÁGI Travel Agency** (Kucsera F utca 15, ☎ 26 310 030).

Named after the painter couple Imre Amos and Anna Margit who lived here, the **Amos and Anna Museum** (Amos and Anna Múzeum) is full of moving paintings that reflect their often troubled lives. Amos died in forced labour on the Russian front in Ukraine. Anna is buried in the

courtyard of the house. *(Bogdányi utca 10.*
🕐 *Fri-Sun: 10am-4pm. Mon-Thu: closed.*
Admission charge.)

The **Barcsay Museum** (Barcsay Múzeum)
houses a collection of fine drawings,
sketches, maps and diagrams by the artist
Jenöö Barcsay who died in 1988. *(Dumtsa*
Jenö utca 10. 🕐 *Tue-Sun: 10am-4pm. Mon:*
closed. Admission charge.)

Károly Ferenczy was one of Hungary's
leading Impressionists and helped to
found the Nagybanya artists' colony at the
turn of the century. A vein of artistic talent
clearly ran through the Ferenczy family
because several of his relatives' works also
hang in the **Ferenczy Museum** (Ferenczy
Múzeum). *(Fő tér 6,* ☎ *26 310 790.* 🕐 *Fri-Sun:*
10am-4pm. Mon-Thu: closed. Admission
charge.)

The **Margit Kovács Museum** (Margit Kovács
Múzeum) is extremely popular and you
may have to queue for some time just to
get through the door. Kovács was an
eminent Hungarian sculptor and ceramics
designer who worked in the middle years
of the 20th century. There is much
evidence in her work of the influence of
Hungarian folk traditions. *(Vastagh György*
utca 1, ☎ *26 310 790.* 🕐 *Apr-Oct: Tue-Sun:*
10am-6pm. Mon: 10am-4pm. Nov-Mar: Mon:
closed. Admission charge.)

Another popular destination in the
countryside is **Lake Balaton**. The biggest
lake in Western Europe, it is surrounded
by rolling, green hills. Its location just 60
miles (100 km) from Budapest makes it
ideal for a day or weekend trip. Public
transport and coach excursions serve the
area well, particularly during the summer.

One of the major resorts here is
Balatonfüred on the northern shore. This
old town has a historic centre and a lively
harbour area, as well as beaches and a
pier. The spa town, which features a
natural spring in the old square, retains
an air of elegance despite the hordes of
tourists.

More lively is the southern-shore resort of
Siófok, the destination of sun-seekers and
party animals. Its lakeside promenade is
lined with restaurants and night spots,
and pleasure cruisers depart from here.

Reflections

'Anyone who wants to
understand Hungary
needs to find the answer
to one great secret: how
is it that this country has
survived at all? ... no
nation is so experienced
in defeat as the
Hungarians' – Istvan
Eörsi, Hungarian
journalist and poet

Dining

Hungarian food is traditionally rich and heavy. The most famous dish is goulash (*gulyás* or *pörkölt*) which is a steaming meat stew spiced with paprika, garlic and herbs. It can be served with rice or small dumplings (*galuska*) and is delicious either for lunch or dinner.

Restaurants in Budapest like to personalise their goulash by varying the ingredients (veal goulash or *borjúpörkölt* is one favourite). There is also a goulash soup (*gulyásleves*) which is very popular.

Meat (*húsetelek*) plays a leading role in Budapest food, from steaks to game, including the sought-after wild boar (*vaddisznó*). Vegetarians are less well provided for.

There are lots of fish dishes, notably carp (*ponty*) and catfish (*harcsaszeletek*), but completely meat-free alternatives can be hard to track down.

Budapest's proximity to Russia means caviar (*kaviar*) appears regularly on starter menus along with another national favourite, goose liver (*libamaj*).

Hungary used to make wine (*bor*) for the elite of the Roman Empire when they controlled this part of Europe. Today, the only really well-known wine is Bull's Blood, which makes a good companion to gamey

Gerbeaud

Vörösmarty tér 7
Ⓜ Vörösmarty tér
☎ 318 1311
🕐 Mon-Sun: 9am-9pm.

Coffee and a croissant at Gerbeaud's, a Hungarian tradition dating from 1870

meats, but there are quite a few other local ones worth trying. A refreshing beer (*sör*) is recommended with goulash.

For diners who make it through to dessert, try the pancakes (*palacsinta*), especially when stuffed with sweet fillings and laced with rum, chocolate and cream.

If it is just a snack you are after, then drop in to one of Budapest's many coffee houses, where you can nibble at cakes and sandwiches, sip an espresso and write your postcards. **Gerbeaud** is the most famous, having been in existence since 1870. It is sumptuously decorated in the original style and incorporates a very popular confectionery shop.

Restaurants are spread evenly throughout the central parts of the city, with clusters in the **Castle District** and on the Pest bank of the **Chain Bridge**. The area of **Inner City Pest** between the river and the **Hungarian National Museum** (page 31) has both expensive and moderately priced places serving mainly non-Magyar foods, including Indian, Thai, Greek, and Korean.

Magyar eateries are everywhere, but most notably in the area of Pest between **Károly körút** and **Erzsebet körút**, the **Castle District** and north **Buda**.

The **Gundel** in City Park is Budapest's most famous, and probably its most expensive, restaurant. It has stood here for more than 100 years and is known for its game and fresh fish dishes. Expect to spend a small fortune on the wine alone. This is the home of the Gundel pancake, a layer of fruit and nuts wrapped in a pancake and smothered in rum and chocolate.

The **New York Kávéház**, despite the name, is a grand Budapest tradition, having served coffee and delicious pastries in its Art Nouveau surroundings for almost a century.

Vegetarian restaurants are rare in Budapest, notable exceptions being the **Govinda** Indian restaurant on Belgrád rakpart on the river and the **Marquis de Salade** on Hájos utca.

Gundel

XIV. Állatkerti körút 2
Ⓜ Széchenyi fürdő
☎ 321 3550
🕐 Mon-Sat: 12noon-3pm and 6.30pm-12midnight. Sun: 11.30am-3pm and 6.30pm-12midnight.

New York Kávéház

VII. Erzsébet körút 9-11
Ⓜ Blaha Lujza tér
☎ 322 3849
🕐 Café: 10am-12midnight.
Restaurant: 12noon-4pm and 6.30pm-12midnight.

Marquis de Salade

VI. Hajós utca 43
Ⓜ Nyugati
☎ 302 4086
🕐 Mon-Sun: 12noon-12midnight.

Shopping

Budapest, like many East European cities that have recently emerged from communism, is on the way up. Each year more and more shops open, capitalising on the increasing affluence of its citizens and the growing tourism market.

It is easy to pick up well-made, authentic Hungarian arts and crafts in shops throughout the city. The prices have until recently been reasonable, but are rising steadily towards western levels as shop-owners realise what tourists are used to paying back home.

Most folk crafts are made by **Folkart**, a state-owned company, and are clearly labelled as such. You will find them for sale in the open markets, the large department stores and the shopping malls, as well as in the smaller, usually more expensive and classier looking shops. Hungary's most famous export, hand-painted Herend pottery, can be found all over town. The widest selection is in the **Herend Shop**.

There is an expanding number of art galleries in Budapest showing and selling paintings, sculptures, photographs and graphic art at fairly competitive prices. Some have shipping services. If you are looking for antiques, however, ask shop owners about exporting them because Hungarian customs rules can be strict. Some shops can deal with the paperwork for you, but for a price.

The main two areas for shopping are the **Castle District**, which has numerous souvenir shops between the museums and the historic medieval houses, and **Váci utca**, a pedestrianised street that runs parallel with the river in Pest between the **Erzsébet** and **Szabadság bridges**.

Kossuth Lajos utca is another key shopping street, running east off the Erzsébet Bridge and dissecting Pest. The open markets are dotted around the city and marked clearly on maps.

Like all other European cities, Budapest has its fair share of American-style shopping malls. The first to open was

---

Herend Shop

V. József Nádor tér 11
Ⓜ Vörösmarty tér
☎ 317 2622
🕐 Mon-Fri: 10am-6pm.
Sat: 9am-1pm.
Sun: closed.

Duna Plaza

XIII. Váci út 178
Ⓜ Gyöngyösi út
☎ 465 1666
🕐 Mon-Fri: 10am-9pm.
Sat-Sun: 10am-7pm.

Kossuth lajos utca

Ⓜ Ferenciek tere

Sugár (☎ *Örs Vezér tere*). **Duna Plaza**, on Váci utca, offers leisure activities as well as a good range of shops and stores.

The malls have little to recommend them when compared to the joys of shopping in Budapest's **open markets**. There are several in central locations and all are fascinating whether you are there to buy, or just to look and take photographs. There are flea markets selling everything from teapots to tambourines to Communist memorabilia to caviar.

The **food markets** are ideal if you are going on a walking tour around the city and want to take a picnic. They teem with giant cheeses, great haunches of meat, and stalls overloaded with fruit and vegetables. Some colourful stalls are draped with strings of bright red and yellow peppers (paprika) tied up and hung out to dry.

Others are rich with the scents from hundreds of bottles of herbs and spices. Some markets now sell a wide range of Asian goods, including restorative balms and ointments. The markets look especially inviting at Christmas, when the stalls are covered with decorations.

A few open markets that are definitely worth a visit are the **Central Market Hall** (Központi Vásárcsarnok) on Vámház körút, the **Market in the Józsefváros** (Józsefvárosi piac), the **Central Market** (Kozponti Vásárcsarnok) on Rákóczi tér, and the **Inner City Market Hall** (Belvárosi Vásárcsarnok) on Hold utca. Haggle over prices and keep your wallet safe as pickpockets are common in these busy places.

Inner City Market Hall

V. Hold utca 13
Ⓜ Arany János
☎ 353 1110
🕐 Mon: 6.30am-5pm.
Tue-Fri: 6.30am-6pm.
Sat: 6.30am-2pm.
Sun: closed.

Market produce

Nightlife

Budai Vigadó

Budapest offers a diversity of after-dark experiences that ranges from a seedy striptease club to a performance by the Hungarian Railway Workers Symphony Orchestra.

Many venues are open throughout the year but others run from September through to late spring. The best way to find out what's on, where and when, is to contact the Hungarian Tourism Office, **Tourinform**, when you arrive. It is also worth scouring the pages of the newspapers and entertainment guides in your hotel.

Opera is affordable and extremely popular and the **Hungarian State Opera House** (Magyar Állami Operaház) is rarely quiet. Always book tickets at least a couple of days in advance if you can, although there are usually some last-minute seats available if you don't mind perching in the high balconies.

There are classical music concerts at a range of venues, from the **Budapest Convention Centre** *(XII. Jagélló út 1-3,* Ⓜ *Moszkva tér,* ☎ *361 2869)* to the more intimate **Béla Bartók Memorial House** (page 44) *(II. Csalán út 29, Moszkva tér,* ☎ *394 2100)*, and the religious settings of the churches of **Matthias** and **St. Stephen** (pages 16 and 25). The **Musica Viva Arts Foundation** should have current details *(*☎ *317 7031)*, or call the venues direct: **Central Theatre** *(VI. Andrássy út 18,* ☎ *312 0000 or 135 9136)*, **National Philharmonic** *(V. Vörösmarty tér 1,* Ⓜ *Vörösmarty tér* ☎ *118 0209)*, **Hungarian State Opera** *(*☎ *332 8197)*.

Folk music is also popular and the Hungarian State Folk Ensemble perform

Tourinform

Sütő utca 2
Ⓜ Deák tér
☎ 317 9800

Hungarian State Opera House

Andrássy út 22
Ⓜ Opera
☎ 332 8197

egularly at the **Budai Vigadó**. Look out for istings in local papers and tourist guides o Folk Dancing Houses, where you can watch dance groups from across Hungary perform in traditional costume. At some venues you will be able to try a step or two yourself in organised lessons led by experienced tutors.

There are several mainstream and fringe theatres that regularly perform classical and modern works, from Shakespeare to experimental theatre. Other venues perform ballet. Newspapers have details of performance schedules.

Check with the theatres or tourist offices that the plays are in English and not Hungarian – unless you are fluent in the native tongue or know the play well the plot will be impossible to follow. The **Merlin Theatre** frequently stages productions in English and German and is the only primarily foreign-language venue in the city, although other theatres may hold the occasional English performance.

The wonderful coffeehouses come alive in the evening when they are frequented by the office crowd undoing their ties and relaxing after a hard day's work, and by travellers meeting to begin a night on the town. In the summer, people sit outside at tables in the street.

Some, like **Café Miro** in Castle District *(I. Uri utca 30, Ⓜ Moszkva tér, ☎ 375 5458)* or the **Astoria Café** in the hotel of the same name in Pest *(V. Kossuth Lajos utca 19-21, Ⓜ Astória, ☎ 318 6265)*, have elegant decors with paintings or bookshelves adorning the walls. Others are more basic, but whichever one you choose strong and delicious coffee will be served.

Budai Vigadó

I. Corvin Ter
Ⓜ Batthyány tér
☎ 201 3766

Merlin Theatre

V. Gerlóczy utca 4
Ⓜ Astoria / Deák tér
☎ 317 9338

Hungarian folk dancing

A pleasure boat on the Danube

Many coffeehouses sell sandwiches and cakes throughout the day. Almost all the coffeehouses are closed by midnight, some by 11pm and a random few by 9pm.

There are plenty of pubs in the city centre and just beyond. Many are themed or based on American, Irish, British or Belgian bars. These are patronised by expatriates as well as tourists, but there are also local establishments where you'll meet Hungarians.

English is not very widely spoken by bar staff, but sign language always seems to work. They may have a menu for drinks as well as food, so you can always smile and point to your choice.

For a taste of Bohemian Budapest nightlife, try the **Wichmann** bar in Pest on Kazinczy utca, between Andrássy utca and Rakóczi utca, where you can rub shoulders with students deep in intellectual conversation and surrounded by bottles of beer.

Budapest has a burgeoning night club scene catering to aficionados of jazz, blues, rock, disco and house music. Most clubs do not get swinging until after midnight and do not close until after dawn. Admission charges to clubs are reasonable by Western European standards. One of the most renowned and popular clubs is **Bahnhof**, which has a railway theme.

Wichmann

VII. Kazinczy utca 55
Ⓜ Deák tér
☎ 321 1897

n the summer there are several outdoor
music festivals. The biggest is the week-
long Sziget Fesztival in August, which
boasts all the usual festival trappings,
namely numerous tents and stages
catering for all manner of musical tastes,
vast quantities of beer and cheap things
to eat.

Budapest has been lost in the wilderness
when it comes to international rock music
concerts and is only now beginning to
attract some big names. Large venues for
rock bands include Petőfi Csarnok in City
Park *(XIV. Városliget, Zichy Mihály út 14, u
Széchenyi Fürdő, ☎ 343 4327)* which has
both an outdoor and an indoor stage. It
has hosted several reasonably famous
Western bands.

Gay and lesbian visitors will find a lively
and friendly scene in the bars, discos and
coffee shops. Quite a few of the thermal
baths are gay rendezvous. The **Capella
Café** is one of the city's best gay clubs,
but is also suitable for a mixed crowd.

Budapest's sex industry is not as blatant
as that of Amsterdam, but is arguably as
big. It is controlled predominantly by
Mafia-style gangs from Russia and Eastern
Europe. Insistent taxi drivers get pocket-
money from enticing tourists into
expensive erotic clubs and bars whose
entrances are guarded by fierce security
guards.

Official, licensed taxis can be hard to pick
out from the swarm of different car
companies touting for your fare, some of
whom are barely legal and will almost
certainly overcharge. Those recommended
are **Fő Taxi** *(☎ 222 2222)* and **Yellow Pages**
(☎ 355 5000).

Several companies run cruises up the
Danube at night, offering marvellous views
of the city's finest buildings. The
embarkation points are quays along the
Belgrad rakpart on the Pest side of the
river. The tourism office will have details of
sailing times and costs.

Budapest has its fair share of casinos, and
for real insomniacs there are several shops
that stay open 24 hours a day selling
mainly convenience goods.

Bahnhof

VI. Váci utca 1
Ⓜ Nyugati

Capella Café

V. Belgrád Rakpart 23
Ⓜ Ferenciek tere
☎ 318 6231

Visitor Information

CHILDREN

Budapest has plenty of attractions for visitors of any age. Children will enjoy the play area in **Jubilee Park** (page 15), the **Children's Railway** (page 22) and the various attractions in **City Park** (page 38), which include the **Budapest Zoo**, the **Municipal Grand Circus** and an amusement area.

Museums of interest to younger visitors include the **Natural History Museum** (page 33) and the **Palace of Wonders** (page 41). A visit to the **Puppet Theatre** (page 35) always goes down well.

CUSTOMS

Import restrictions are: **Tobacco**: 250 cigarettes or 100 cigars; **Alcohol**: 2 litres of wine plus 1 litre of spirits. These apply to travellers over sixteen years of age.

Items of cultural heritage can be removed from the country provided an export permit is granted. Permission must be applied for at one of the Budapest national museums.

EMERGENCIES

Dial ☎ 107 for the police, ☎ 105 for the fire service and ☎ 104 for an ambulance.

The Hungarian flag

ELECTRIC CURRENT

Electricity in Hungary runs on 220V with a two-prong plug.

HEALTH AND SAFETY

Emergency medical treatment is free for visitors. Nevertheless, everyone should take out comprehensive travel insurance that includes medical coverage.

As in any popular tourist destination, take extra care of your belongings in the busiest spots, as pickpockets are becoming ever more common.

HOTELS

Below is a selection of hotels for various budgets in the centre of Budapest.

Buda

Hilton *(I. Hess András tér 1-3,* Ⓜ *Moszkva tér,* ☎ *488 6600.)* Wonderful views and luxury service. 👛 👛 👛 👛 👛

Gellért *(Szent Gellért tér 1,* Ⓜ *Kálvin tér,* ☎ *385 2200.)* An elegant spa hotel, recently renovated. 👛 👛 👛 👛

Victoria *(Bem rkp 11,* ☎ *457 8080.)* Overlooking the Chain Bridge, the Victoria is within easy reach of the major tourist sites. 👛 👛 👛 👛

Alba *(Apor Péter u. 3,* Ⓜ *Batthyány tér,* ☎ *375 9244.)* A neat, Swiss-owned hotel in a cobbled street within minutes of the Castle Hill. 👛 👛 👛

Citadella *(Citadella sétány,* ☎ *466 5794.)* A great value, well located hotel with plenty of facilities. 👛

Pest

Hotel Intercontinental *(Apáczai Csere János utca 12-14,* Ⓜ *Vörösmarty tér,* ☎ *317 7269.)* Good service, a wonderful restaurant and easy access to the sights of Pest. 👛 👛 👛 👛 👛

Atrium Hyatt *(Roosevelt tér,* Ⓜ *Vörösmarty tér,* ☎ *266 1234.)* Spacious, luxurious and centrally located rooms with Danube views. 👛 👛 👛 👛 👛

Taverna *(Váci u. 20,* Ⓜ *Ferenciek tere,* ☎ *338 3522.)* Superbly located in the main shopping area. 👛 👛 👛 👛

Pannonia Hotel Nemzeti *(József krt. 4,* Ⓜ *Blaha Lujza,* ☎ *303 9310.)* A grand old hotel with modern conveniences. 👛 👛 👛

Radio Inn *(Benczúr u. 19,* Ⓜ *Bajza utca,* ☎ *342 8347.)* Close to the City Park, this hotel has spacious apartments at a reasonable price. 👛 👛

LANGUAGE

The Hungarian language is totally unrelated to the languages in the countries surrounding it, having only tenuous links with Finnish and Estonian.

ETIQUETTE

If you can overcome the language barrier (page 58), Hungarians are friendly and courteous and eager to help with directions.

Although smoking is banned on public transport and in places such as theatres, it is widespread everywhere else.

Be sure to greet shopkeepers, waiters etc. when entering or leaving their premises. Not doing so is seen as terribly rude.

Many younger Hungarians and those in the tourist industry speak good English or German.

Hungarians are proud of their language and love to hear foreigners making an effort to speak it.

Hello	*Jo nápot*
Goodbye	*Viszontlátásra*
Excuse me	*Bocsánat*
Yes	*Igen*
No	*Nem*
Please	*Kérem*
Thank you	*Köszönöm*
Do you speak English?	*Beszél angolul?*
I don't understand	*Nem értem*
Where is...?	*Hol van...?*
Entrance	*Bejárat*
Exit	*Kijárat*
Open	*Nyitva*
Closed	*Zárva*

Hungarian names are written or said with the surname first and forename second.

A post box

LUGGAGE STORAGE

You can put baggage into storage at the stations **Nyugati** *(VI. Nyugati tér, ☎ 349 0115)* and **Keleti** *(VIII. Baross tér, ☎ 313 6835)* for between 120-240Ft per item. **Déli** station *(I. Alkotás út, ☎ 375 6293)* has a brand new computerised, multilingual left-luggage facility costing 120Ft per day.

The **bus terminal** at Erzsébét tér *(☎ 317 2562)* has slightly cheaper rates.

MAIL / POST

The **main post**

ffice is at Petőfi Sándor utca 17-19 and s open Monday to Friday 8am-6pm and Saturday 8am-2pm. Poste Restante letters should be addressed here.

t is more usual to take letters to a post office to be stamped and posted, rather han putting them in one of the few red post boxes in the street. Hotels will often post your letters for you.

MONEY

The Hungarian forint (Ft) comes in denominations of 1, 2, 5, 10, 20 and 100 coins and 100, 200, 500, 1,000, 5,000 and 10,000 notes.

When changing money, which can be done at banks, hotels and bureaux de change, keep all receipts to facilitate changing money back at the end of your holiday. Black market exchange is still possible but not advisable.

Travellers' cheques can be changed in banks and at hotels but not in shops and restaurants.

Credit cards, especially Visa, Mastercard and American Express, are widely accepted in hotels, large stores and bigger restaurants.

OPENING HOURS

Banks – Standard opening hours are 9am to 2pm Monday to Thursday and until 1pm on Friday.

Bars / Restaurants – Pubs and bars tend to open until midnight or 2am. Restaurants usually stop serving before midnight.

Museums / Galleries – Museums are usually closed on Mondays. This guide lists individual opening times under each museum's entry.

Shops – Business hours are generally 9am-6pm Monday to Friday, and 9am or 10am to 2pm on Saturday, if at all. 24-hour shops are becoming more common.

SPECIAL TRAVELLERS

Disabled – Contact the Hungarian Disabled Association *(III. San Marco utca 6, ☐ 368 1758)* for help getting around this rather wheelchair-unfriendly city.

LOST PROPERTY

Contact the central lost property office, **Talát Tárgyak Központi Hivatala** *(Erzsébet tér 5, ☎ 317 2318)* about items lost anywhere other than on public transport. Railway stations and taxi companies have their own lost property offices.

Elderly – Where specified in this guide, *for less* discounts are available on top of reduced senior prices.

Students – Concessions are available at many attractions and museums when acceptable ID, such as an ISIC card, is produced. Where specified in this guide, **for less** discounts are available on top of the normal student discount.

Gay – There is an ever-growing gay and lesbian scene in the city, despite the fact that Hungarian culture has rather a conventional outlook on such matters. The monthly publication **Mások** is available at news-stands and contains listings, contact informations and classified ads of interest to gay and lesbian residents and visitors.

TAXES

Everything is subject to VAT. Foreign tourists can claim VAT back on single items costing more than 25,000Ft within 183 days of leaving the country, provided the item is exported within 90 days of purchase. Contact the **Foreigner's Refund Office** *(APEH Budapest Directorate, XI. Bartó Béla út 156, ☎ 203 0888)*.

TELEPHONES

Old coin-operated telephones are being phased out with the modernisation of the Hungarian telecommunications system, which is also leading to a gradual change to telephone numbers. Those beginning with 1 will begin with either 2 or 3 in the near future. Phonecards can be bought from post offices, metro stations and shops such as tobacconists.

To ring Hungarian numbers outside Budapest you must dial ☎ 06 and then the area code and telephone number. The area code for Budapest is ☎ 1.

For the operator, dial ☎ 191 and for the international operator, dial ☎ 190.

TOURIST INFORMATION / LISTINGS

Tourinform is centrally located in Pest at Sütő utca 2 *(☎ 317 9800)*. Friendly, English speaking staff can help you with travel plans, entertainment listings, maps and advice, but they do not offer any booking services.

PACKING

The temperature in Budapest ranges from over 30ºC (86ºF) in the height of summer and well below freezing for long periods in the winter. Even in midwinter, layers of clothing is better than one thick jumper, as the heating inside buildings is often fierce.

To book tours and for help with accommodation, contact **Ibusz** *(V. Petőfi tér 3, ☎ 388 5707).*

TOURS

Boats – Boat tours are a great way to see the famous Blue Danube and are especially rewarding at night when the city is illuminated. Most hotels can provide information about the companies which organise boat tours both in and outside the city.

Bus – Budapest is a relatively small city and can be easily explored on foot. However, **Ibusz** offers bus tours in air-conditioned coaches. They include folklore-themed tours and a 3-hour orientation tour of the city costing about 3,600Ft. Buses leave from the bus terminal at Erzsébet tér, and some offer a hotel pick-up service. For a full list of tours, pick up a brochure in your hotel or at the Ibusz office.

Walking Tours – **Chosen Tours** offer escorted walking tours with a Jewish theme, currently starting at 10.30am every day except Saturday. The tour departs from outside the Central Synagogue (page 28) and costs about 2,200Ft.

Outside Budapest – the Danube Bend is easily accessible by bus or train and is one of the most beautiful parts of the country. Regular boat trips from the city serve the area in the summer. You can find details about these trips at the tourist information offices.

TIPPING

Restaurants – round up the bill or leave a tip of about 10% to supplement waiting staffs' measly pay.

Taxis – it is customary to round the fare up.
Toilets – most public toilets have attendants and a tip of about 20Ft is expected.

A Budapest policeman

The metro

Lake Balaton serves as the seaside in this landlocked country, and is just a 60-mile (100-km) drive away. It can be reached by bus or train, and by organised coach excursion in the summer.

TRANSPORT AROUND THE CITY

Metro – the Budapest underground railway is the most popular form of transport and serves all the main points of interest in the city. It has only three lines which meet at Deák tér. The metro starts running at 4.30am and stops at about 11.30pm.

Tickets can be bought at stations, at tram stops or on news-stands. A single ticket is 90Ft, and a day pass is 700Ft. You can also buy 3-stop, 5-stop or weekly tickets, which work out cheaper.

Validate metro tickets before you board the train on the blue and red lines and on the trains themselves on the yellow line.

Buses – Buses are more useful for getting out of the centre of the city or for night journeys. They are more confusing to use than the metro, as they tend to skip stops.

Validate bus tickets, which can be bought from the same places as metro tickets, in the red machines by the door as you board. Ring the bell above the door to disembark.

Trams – These are easy to use but, like

TRANSPORT FROM THE AIRPORT

Ferihegy airport is 14 miles (22 km) from the city. LRI, the Budapest Airport Authority, run the **Airport Minibus** service, which takes between half and hour and an hour. It will take you to any address in the city and costs 1,200Ft. For the return journey, book a day in advance (☎ 296 8555).

A cheaper option is to take the LRI-run **Airport-Centrum** bus, which goes to the central Erzsébet tér bus station every half an hour for about 500Ft.

uses, tickets are valid for one journey
only without a change. Validate them as
you board.

Trams stop at every stop, unlike buses,
which makes it easier to keep track of
where you are.

Taxis – Notorious for swindling foreigners,
taxis are not usually the best transport
option in Budapest. However, **Fő Taxi** and
Yellow Pages are recognised firms which
offer competitive transportation.

Trolleybuses – Pest alone is served by a
small network of trolleybuses. Like buses,
they may skip stops and make it hard to
know where you are.

Maps and timetables of all the forms of
public transport in Budapest can be
purchased from metro stations and tourist
information offices.

USEFUL TELEPHONE NUMBERS

Tourinform Tourist Centre ☎ 317 9800

Ferihegy Airport Switchboard ☎ 296 9696

International Rail Information ☎ 461 5500

Domestic Rail Information 24-hour service
461 5400

Erzsébet tér coach station ☎ 317 2318

Fő Taxi ☎ 222 2222

Directory Enquiries (domestic) ☎ 198

Directory Enquiries (foreign) ☎ *199*

CREDITS

Principal photography:
Mecky Fögeling,
Photobank.

Front cover photograph:
Mecky Fögeling.

A tram

Index

Budapest History Museum

2 admissions for the price of 1 at the **Budapest History Museum** (page 10)

Valid from October 1, 1999

National Gallery

2 admissions for the price of 1 at the **National Gallery** (page 11)

Valid from October 1, 1999

Pál Molnár-C. Studio-Museum

2 admissions for the price of 1 at the **Pál Molnár-C. Studio Museum** (page 16)

Valid from October 1, 1999

Catacombs

2 tours for the price of 1 at the **Catacombs** (applies for day or night **(Tour I)** only) (page 18)

Valid from October 1, 1999

St. Stephen's Basilica

2 admissions for the price of 1 at **St. Stephen's Basilica** (page 25)

Valid from October 1, 1999

Opera House

2 tours for the price of 1 at the **Opera House** (page 27)

Valid from March 1, 1999

E kupon tulajdonosa az alábbi kedvezményekre jogosult a **Budapesti Történelmi Múzeumban** (old.10):

Kettőt Egyert: Egy belépő megvásárlásával a következő jegy ingyenes.

E kupon tulajdonosa az alábbi kedvezményekre jogosult a **Nemzeti Galéria** (old.11):

Kettőt Egyert: Egy belépő megvásárlásával a következő jegy ingyenes.

E kupon tulajdonosa az alábbi kedvezményekre jogosult a **Molnár-C. Pál Muterem-Múzeum** (old.16):

Kettőt Egyert: Egy belépő megvásárlásával a következő jegy ingyenes.

E kupon tulajdonosa az alábbi kedvezményekre jogosult a **Catacombs** (old.18):

Kettőt Egyert: Egy idegenvezető által vezetett túra megváltása esetén a következő túra ingyenes.

E kupon tulajdonosa az alábbi kedvezményekre jogosult a **Szent István Bazilika** (old.25):

Kettőt Egyert: Egy belépő megvásárlásával a következő jegy ingyenes.

E kupon tulajdonosa az alábbi kedvezményekre jogosult a **Opera House** (old.27):

Kettőt Egyert: Egy idegenvezető által vezetett túra megváltása esetén a következő túra ingyenes.

Museum of Applied Arts

2 admissions for the price of 1 at the **Museum of Applied Arts** (page 33)

Valid from October 1, 1999

Natural History Museum

2 admissions for the price of 1 at the **Natural History Museum** (page 33)

Valid from October 1, 1999

Franz Liszt Museum

2 tours for the price of 1 at the **Franz Liszt Museum** (page 35)

Valid from October 1, 1999

Kodály Memorial Museum

2 admissions for the price of 1 at the **Kodály Memorial Museum** (page 36)

Valid from October 1, 1999

Museum of Fine Arts

2 admissions for the price of 1 at the **Museum of Fine Arts** (page 37)

Valid from October 1, 1999

Kunsthalle (Műcsarnok)

2 admissions for the price of 1 at the **Kunsthalle (Műcsarnok)** (page 38)

Valid from October 1, 1999

E kupon tulajdonosa az alábbi kedvezményekre jogosult a **Iparművészeti Múzeum** (old.33):

Kettőt Egyert: Egy belépő megvásárlásával a következő jegy ingyenes.

E kupon tulajdonosa az alábbi kedvezményekre jogosult a **Természettudományi Múzeum** (old.33):

Kettőt Egyert: Egy belépő megvásárlásával a következő jegy ingyenes.

E kupon tulajdonosa az alábbi kedvezményekre jogosult a **Liszt Ferenc Múzeum** (old.35):

Kettőt Egyert: Egy idegenvezető által vezetett túra megváltása esetén a következő túra ingyenes.

E kupon tulajdonosa az alábbi kedvezményekre jogosult a **Kodály Emlék Múzeum** (old.37):

Kettőt Egyert: Egy belépő megvásárlásával a következő jegy ingyenes.

E kupon tulajdonosa az alábbi kedvezményekre jogosult a **Szépmüvészeti Múzeum** (old.37):

Kettőt Egyert: Egy belépő megvásárlásával a következő jegy ingyenes.

E kupon tulajdonosa az alábbi kedvezményekre jogosult a **Műcsarnok** (old.38):

Kettőt Egyert: Egy belépő megvásárlásával a következő jegy ingyenes.

Budapest Zoo

2 admissions for the price of 1 at
the **Budapest Zoo** (page 39)

Valid from October 1, 1999

Transport Museum

2 admissions for the price of 1 at
the
Transport Museum (page 41)

Valid from October 1, 1999

Palace of Wonders

2 admissions for the price of 1 at
the
Palace of Wonders (page 41)

Valid from October 1, 1999

Aquincum Museum and Roman Town

2 tours for the price of 1 at the
Aquincum Museum and Roman Town (page 43)

Valid from October 1, 1999

Kiscelli Museum

2 admissions for the price of 1 at
the
Kiscelli Museum (page 45)

Valid from October 1, 1999

Szelmő-hegy Caves

2 admissions for the price of 1 at
the **Szelmő-hegy Caves** (page 45)

Valid from October 1, 1999

E kupon tulajdonosa az alábbi
kedvezményekre jogosult a
Állatkert (old.39):

Kettőt Egyert: Egy belépő
megvásárlásával a következő
jegy ingyenes.

E kupon tulajdonosa az alábbi
kedvezményekre jogosult a
Közlekedési Múzeum (old.41):

Kettőt Egyert: Egy belépő
megvásárlásával a következő
jegy ingyenes.

E kupon tulajdonosa az alábbi
kedvezményekre jogosult a
Csodák Palotája (old.41):

Kettőt Egyert: Egy belépő
megvásárlásával a következő
jegy ingyenes.

E kupon tulajdonosa az alábbi
kedvezményekre jogosult a
Aquincumi Múzeum (old.43):

Kettőt Egyert: Egy idegenvezető
által vezetett túra megváltásá
esetén a következő túra ingyenes.

E kupon tulajdonosa az alábbi
kedvezményekre jogosult a
Kiscelli Muzeum (old.45):

Kettőt Egyert: Egy belépő
megvásárlásával a következő
jegy ingyenes.

E kupon tulajdonosa az alábbi
kedvezményekre jogosult a
Szelmő-hegy barlang (old.45):

Kettőt Egyert: Egy belépő
megvásárlásával a következő
jegy ingyenes.

Pálvölgyi Caves

2 admissions for the price of 1 at
the **Pálvölgyi Caves** (page 45)

Valid from October 1, 1999

Customer Response Card

We would like to hear your comments about the
Budapest for less Compact Guide so that we can
improve it. Please complete the information below
and mail this card. One card will be picked out at
random to win a free holiday.
No stamp is required, either in Hungary or your own
country.

Name: ....

Address: ....

Tel. no.: ....

If you bought the book, where did you buy it from?..

....

If you were given the book, which tour operator
gave it to you? ....

Number of people travelling in your party? ....

How many days were you in Budapest? ....

Did you like the guidebook?...

What did you like about it?..

....

Would you recommend it to a friend?...........................

Would you be more interested in a tour operator's
package if you knew it included the **Budapest for
less Compact Guide**? ....

....

Any other comments..

....

....

....

....

....

E kupon tulajdonosa a következő kedvezmények illetik a **Pálvölgyi barlang** (old.45):

Kettőt Egyert: Egy belépő megvásárlásával a következő jegy ingyenes.

NE PAS AFFRANCHIR

NO STAMP REQUIRED

REPONSE PAYEE
GRANDE-BRETAGNE

Metropolis International (UK) Limited
222 Kensal Road
LONDON, GREAT BRITAIN
W10 5BN

By air mail
Par avion

IBRS/CCRI NUMBER: PHQ-D/2560/W